101
Hotel Rooms

101

Corinna Kretschmar-Joehnk
Peter Joehnk

Hotel Rooms

BRAUN

Content

Preface
by Corinna Kretschmar-Joehnk and Peter Joehnk

101 Hotel Rooms was born out of our desire to make public the latter part of nearly 30 years of experience in hotel design. Time and again we have re-invented the hotel room, in very different layouts, responding to a variety of requirements, and for a diverse list of hotel operators.

At some point we realised that we weren't willing to let this know-how moulder away in drawers and computer files, but wanted to make it available to the general public. That's how we came to produce this book showcasing a wide variety of takes on the recurring theme of the hotel room. We hope that in doing so we have created something that will be a valuable reference for architects, interior designers, investors, project developer, hoteliers and, of course, students. *101 Hotel Rooms* presents creative solutions that were designed to fit a broad range of floor plans.

Whether our assignments involved resort, city, luxury, or budget hotels, we have pondered and found solutions to nearly every kind of requirement in this sector. This book compiles, condenses and presents these solutions in a clear and attractive format.

Using a consistent design layout that includes floor plans, concept drawings, perspectives and photographs, we show the reader not only functional solutions applied to a wide variety of interior spaces, but also an abundance of different design solutions for hotel rooms and bathrooms. At JOI-Design we don't follow a particular house style. Rather, we focus on finding the perfect solution for each individual project. As a result, our portfolio covers the broadest possible spectrum – from the classic design of a Viennese palace hotel, to prize-winning design hotels and highly successful spa hotels.

From hundreds of completed and ongoing projects we have put together a stunningly diverse collection of designs. We hope you will get as much enjoyment from perusing these designs as we got from creating them.

101 Hotel Rooms

'Adaptable'
Guest Room Concept

Room Concept
Hotel Category: ★ ★ ★ ★ ★
Hotel Type: City hotel
The Brief: New construction / Designing a concept for a guest room
Floor area incl. bathrooms: 30.30 m²

The diagonal slant of the bathroom enclosure into the room creates tension, both horizontally and vertically. This fluid sculptural feature is balanced and accommodated by the long swinging arc of a sideboard along the opposite wall. Integrated into the sideboard is a mobile desk. In recent years the way hotel desks are used has changed radically. Today, digital nomads travel everywhere with a portable computer and want to be reachable at all times. Wi-Fi is a necessity, prompting a common-sense approach to the use of space. Given that a flatscreen television can be connected to a laptop, what could be more sensible than to do away with the rigidity of a fixed location for the desk? This concept proposes a flexible table/desk that can be moved anywhere in the room, even next to the bed or in front of the armchair. Once work is done, the amorphously shaped desk can be fitted back into its niche in the sideboard. This pioneering design idea was a response to numerous wishes by guests.

An interactive room and a desk on the move.

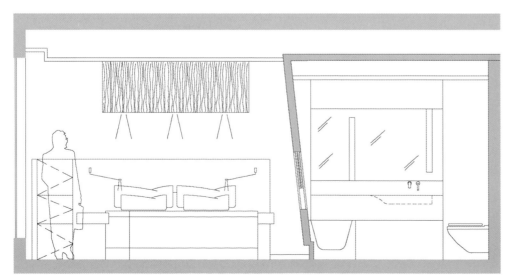

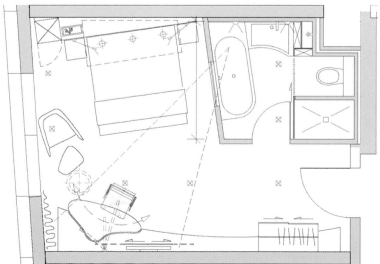

Alpina Ferienlodge
St. Oswald / Austria

Apartment Concept
Hotel Category: ★ ★ ★ ★
Hotel Type: Holiday Village
The Brief: Conversion of existing lodges / Designing a concept for an apartment
Floor area incl. bathrooms: 55.58 m²

Located in a beautiful Alpine village far above the tree line, the cosy design of these gorgeous wooden cottages will delight guests – the Alpina Ferienlodge in St. Oswald is everything an Alpine tourist could wish for.

The cottages are a testament to the beauty of traditional Alpine designs, and their refurbishment presented a special challenge. Rather than masquerading as an original interior that is more than 100 years old, the new room concept preserves the charm of the existing architecture and marries it with a sleek new look – a traditional design that has moved with the times.

The original wooden walls and ceilings were retained, along with many of the old furnishings, while the accessories, fabrics, lighting elements and new furnishings are resolutely twenty-first-century designs. The result is an unaffected design that blends the old and the new in an atmosphere of timeless elegance. The white designer armchair, the old wooden table, and the grey "state-of-the-art" fabric upholstery on the old corner sofa are all perfectly matched to this cosy old "Alpine hut".

Rustic Alpine traditions married to a modern design concept.

'Art Déco'
Guest Room Concept

Guest Room Concept
Hotel Category: ★ ★ ★ ★ ★
Hotel Type: City hotel
The Brief: New building / Develop a
design concept for a deluxe room
Floor area excl. bathrooms: 20.28 m²

This design will charm guests with its consistent application of a classic leitmotif: the lily. In a fast-paced age of sensory overload, the elegant design of this room offers guests a place to relax and unwind. Drawing on designs from earlier epochs, its warm colour scheme creates an atmosphere that is timeless yet very contemporary.

An outsized lily adorns the carpeting and this motif is reproduced across a variety of surfaces in a tone-in-tone colour scheme. Glossy pilaster strips on the wardrobe elegantly set off the large floral print. Wherever you look, lilies abound: whether as an inlay on the headboard or a silhouette cut-out on the side table. Easily missed at a glance, the ornate floral engravings on the surfaces of the desk add a tactile dimension. The wallpapering – the source of inspiration for this design – wraps around the room to complete this extravagant exploration of the floral theme. The subtle metallic nuances of the wallpapering add a hint of Modernism and evoke a contemporary atmosphere.

A contemporary design that reflects on times past.

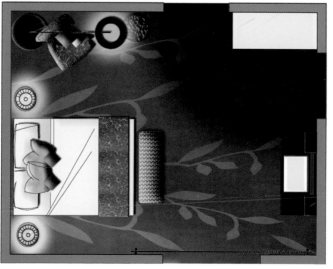

Beach Hotel
Ulcinj / Montenegro

Room Concept
Hotel Category: ★ ★ ★ ★
Hotel Type: Resort hotel
The Brief: New building / Create a design concept for a room
Floor area incl. bathrooms: 42.44 m^2

A balanced design – placing the fixtures at a slight angle to the entrance counters the floor plan's "tunnel effect" and opens up the room. The angle guides guests into the room, turning the bed slightly towards the sofa arrangement and the window. The layout subtly shields the quiet zone around the bed from the reception area, which features a wardrobe, bathroom and desk. The hotel is situated directly on the ocean promenade and the room enjoys gorgeous sea views – this is where you want to be! The balcony forms an integral element of the living area and guests will enjoy relaxing here with a good book or a glass of wine. The natural tile flooring is an ideal solution for sandy feet and creates a pleasant indoor climate – two tiling styles create natural thru-zones around the quiet areas. A warm red tone cuts through the bright colour scheme and marks off the relaxation areas.

Angular design – a room opens up to the sea.

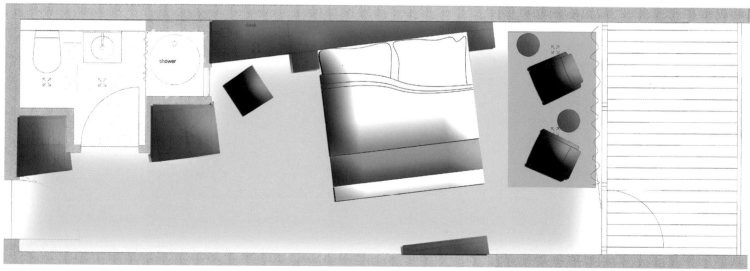

Boardinghouse
Munich / Germany

Apartment Concept
Hotel Category: ★ ★ ★ – ★ ★ ★ ★
Hotel Type: City hotel
The Brief: New building / Create a design concept for apartments with an extended stay
Floor area incl. bathrooms: 27.07 m²

A home away from home: the hotel room that's not a hotel room. This is a place where guests can really make themselves at home. The design cleverly disguises the fact that this is indeed a hotel: the wall unit offers plenty of space for guests to lay out their own books, photographs and personal belongings. A tidy room is a room worth living in – there is enough space for everything here!

The carefully integrated sofa niche provides guests with a place to rest and relax. The sloping cutaway of the wall unit enhances this effect and evokes associations with a gabled attic studio. A desk chair and

ottoman can also be pulled up to accommodate guests. Equipped with the latest hi-tech gadgetry, the timeless elegance of the desk makes it an integral element in this ensemble and its rustic Bavarian style adds a dash of local flair to the apartment. Located close to the entrance, the glass exterior of the bathroom forms an exciting contrast – an open design for individual living.

A room with home décor – next-generation serviced apartments.

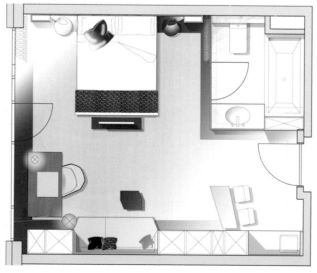

Boutiquehotel 'Le Clervaux'
Clerf, Luxembourg

Suite Concept
Hotel Category: ★ ★ ★ ★ superior
Hotel Type: Boutique + Design Hotel
The Brief: Complete refurbishment /
Designing a concept for a suite
Floor area incl. bathrooms: 42.44 m²

Located between Clervaux's two central squares in the shadow of the mighty castle, this hotel is housed in what was once one of the town's foremost villas. Following a longer closure this grand old lady of Clervaux is set to throw open her doors again – an awoken Sleeping Beauty that will delight and enchant guests with its new design!

The project will entail the creation of approximately 35 suites in the old building, which will be connected to the existing hotel by a bridge. This design seeks to preserve the character of this historical private villa while combining it with contemporary furnishings and transparency provided by semi-satin glazing and a unique shared fireplace that joins the bedroom and living room (the latter can be easily closed off should guests wish to be alone).

Spacious baths, separate toilets, walk-in wardrobes, fireplaces and traditional rooms furnished in a sophisticated urban style provide a luxurious setting for a wellness retreat or a business meeting in 'Le Clervaux'!

Experience history in a contemporary lifestyle environment.

Budget Hotel
Guest Room Concept

Room Concept

Hotel Category: ★ ★ – ★ ★ ★

Hotel Type: Budget hotel

The Brief: Comprehensive renovation of all locations worldwide / Guest room design

Floor area incl. bathrooms: 15.93 m²

This draft concept for a major international brand will set new standards in budget hospitality.

Creating a spacious ambience within a small room is an essential element of budget hospitality design. Here the glazed exterior of the shower links the bathroom to the living space, opening up the room and creating an alcove that snugly accommodates the desk. The design is to be used in a wide range of international settings, and so ease of customisation is an important factor. A simple solution enables the room design to be easily adapted to regional sensibilities and styles: a decorative panel wraps around the room, flowing upwards from the headboard, crossing the ceiling and descending the opposite wall, framing the TV panel before meeting the floor. The wallpapered panel can be decorated with a plain, abstract pattern, a monochrome design, or even one of a range of photographic wall murals.

The decorative panel is a defining element within the room and the choice of motif creates the atmosphere in a design that uses standardised furnishings, enabling hotel operators to enjoy all the benefits of serial production.

A room that can be found all over the world – but different each time.

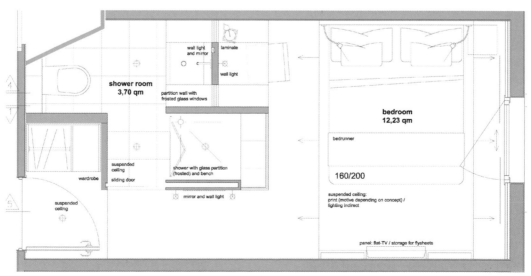

shower room
3,70 qm

wall light
and mirror

laminate

wall light

partition wall with
frosted glass windows

bedroom
12,23 qm

bedrunner

suspended
ceiling

wardrobe

sliding door

shower with glass partition
(frosted) and bench

160/200

suspended
ceiling

mirror and wall light

suspended ceiling:
print (motive depending on concept) /
lighting indirect

panel: flat-TV / storage for flysheets

Room Concept
Hotel Category: ★ ★ – ★ ★ ★
Hotel Type: Budget hotel
The Brief: Comprehensive renovation of
all locations worldwide /
Guest room design
Floor area incl. bathrooms: 15.93 m²

Adaptability is in demand and the trend to-ward an intelligent mix continues. Whether flying with a discount airline and staying in a luxury hotel, or flying business-class to a budget hotel people are cheerfully mixing modes of transportation and accommoda-tion. As a result, the budget hotel sector is experiencing a major upswing, especially in the urban and business sectors. Many travellers allow for a couple days of luxury vacation, splashing out on cuisine, well-ness experiences and other "packages", but spending the night in a budget hotel. The hotel room should also be designed for this purpose. If you occasionally need more space and would like to open up luggage on a luggage stand, the stand can be drawn out of its niche into the room. Alternatively, this may serve as further seating for a ca-sual tête-à-tête or as a footrest if you wish to stretch out and put one's feet up. Even the shower cubicle is adaptable: a ledge serves a double purpose a bench to sit on or as place to put shower toiletries.

The intelligent room: adaptable utility in a tight space.

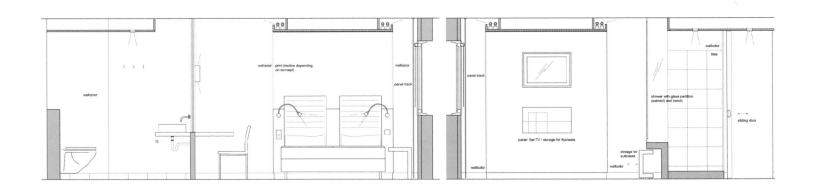

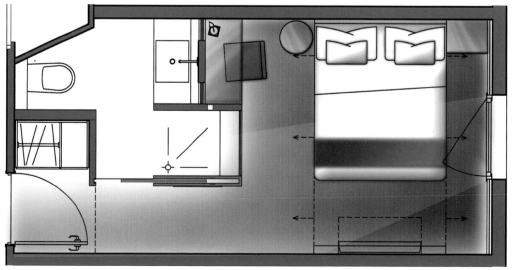

'C-Cube'
Guest Room Concept

Room Concept
Hotel Category: ★ ★ ★ ★ – ★ ★ ★ ★ ★
Hotel Type: City hotel
The Brief: Complete Refurbishment /
Develop a design concept
for a deluxe room
Floor area incl. bathrooms: 18.82 m²

With separate living and sleeping areas, this small room has all the style of a suite. The sweeping curve of the sculptural C – fashioned from light maple wood – forms a platform for the sleeping area and dominates the visual design. No railing is necessary as the platform is bordered by an exterior wall and a desk. The television is embedded in a large glass panel facing the bed.

This visually stunning, young design exudes an aura of safety and modern esprit. Necessity is the mother of invention – in this case the narrow floor plan made it necessary to position the bed and desk side by side rather than one behind the other. The grand gesture of the sculptural C balances the bed, which would otherwise dominate the room.

The spatial constraints also required that the wardrobe be positioned towards the rear of the room against the bathroom wall. The unusual functional layout is balanced by the oversized headboard and canopy, while the sculptural C platform creates a visual identity that is distinctive and memorable.

Grand gestures in a small room.

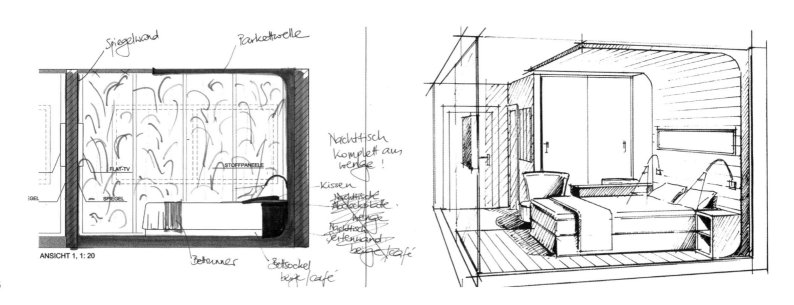

ANSICHT 1, 1: 20

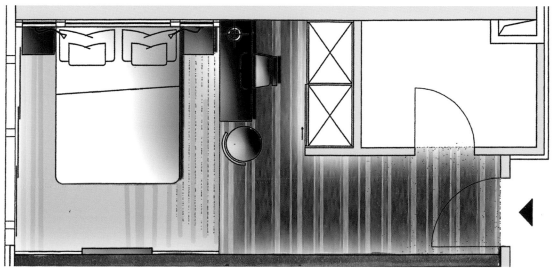

The Charleston
Berlin / Germany

Room Concept
Hotel Category: ★ ★ ★ ★ ★ superior
Hotel Type: Conference hotel
The Brief: New building / Create a design concept for a room
Floor area incl. bathrooms: 29.69 m²

The building's exterior features a contemporary design and clear lines. But can the modern vocabulary of this new concept match the classic splendour of Berlin's most iconic hotels? It's a challenge that calls for an innovative approach: today's guests want something more, they want an emotional experience with an authentic flavour. They want to experience something real, something that they can tell their friends and colleagues about.
The solution: a cutting edge design with a story that appeals to the emotions! Berlin is once again the capital of Germany. The golden age of this grand metropolis was in the Roaring Twenties, when all of Berlin seemed to kick up its heels to the sound of the Charleston as celebrities flocked to the city's Grand Hotels, many of which still exist!
The interior design translates the charm of that era into a modern look: the lines and materials are suggestive of the swinging movements of dancers, evoking images of pearl necklaces, and feather boas. Long live the Charleston!

A dynamic and elegant design with plenty of history: The Roaring Twenties are back.

Cityhotel
Cologne / Germany

Room Concept
Hotel Category: ★ ★ ★ ★
Hotel Type: Business hotel
The Brief: New building / Create a design concept for a room
Floor area incl. bathrooms: 28.83 m²

Black and white meets reed green: the austere colour scheme creates an elegant and fresh look. This is a place where business guests can unwind, recharge their batteries, and prepare for their next meeting. The refreshing effect of the green accents will sooth raw nerves at the end of a busy day. Natural imagery infuses the room with a sense of lightness.

All-round comfort: an oval ottoman serves as a side table, footrest and tray in one. This homely accessory contrasts neatly with the reserved style of the design. A corner unit houses a collection of glasses and a coffee percolator – all that guests will need for a nightcap or an early morning coffee. The wardrobe sports an intelligent open design – with an average stay of just 1.3 days, guests are likely to leave something behind in a closed wardrobe. Last but not least, the bathroom: spacious showers are the next big thing. In order to give guests the best of both worlds, this bath features a spacious shower zone.

Pin stripes: a city hotel in business attire with a splash of green.

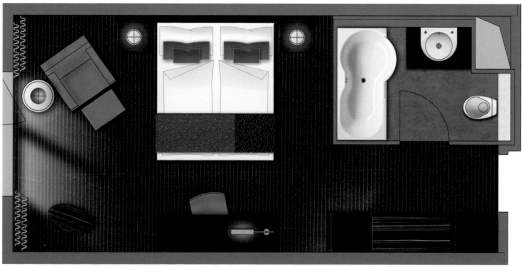

Citytower
Würzburg / Germany

Room Concept
Hotel Category: ★ ★ ★ ★
Hotel Type: City hotel
The Brief: Conversion of an existing building / Create a design concept for a room
Floor area incl. bathrooms: 31.11 m²

Transparency and an airy style balance the strong lines of the building's glass façade in this design: a conversion project that is set to transform the Citytower into a hotel. The design language balances the interior and exterior, subtly translating elements of the existing architecture in the process: the flowing line of the bathroom's exterior wall reflects the curvature of the tower's exterior – the reflective glass surfaces and bright materials capture its transparency. In a new spatial experience, the bathtub is encased in a cubic form that extends into the living area, opening up the room and flooding the bathroom with daylight. The

bed is tucked into the niche created by the bathtub. Guests spend much of their time in bed, so the traditionally blank surface of the ceiling was replaced with a visual lullaby: a work of art that will inspire and calm the mind. This is a room for individualists with a panoramic view of the city: bright, open, inspiring.

A perfect balance – an interior design that matches the façade.

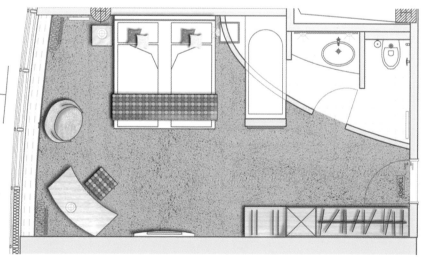

Congress Hotel
Berlin / Germany

Room Concept
Hotel Category: ★ ★ ★ ★
Hotel Type: Business hotel
The Brief: Complete refurbishment /
Create a design concept for a room
Floor area incl. bathrooms: 25.11 m²

Situated close to Berlin's Gendarmen-markt, this hotel is set to receive a make-over that will capture the spirit of this auspicious location and fulfil the needs of a discerning clientele: a contemporary interpretation of classical style.

In this concept design motifs from yester-year act as a bridge to this historical site, while a striking blend of contemporary materials and furnishings makes for an unmistakably up-to-date design. Just like Berlin, this distinctive interior is full of ex-citing contrasts – an appetizer for newcom-ers to Germany's illustrious capital.

One particularly convenient feature is a motion sensor that automatically illumi-nates an eye-catching chandelier as guests enter the room, thus flaunting the stylish design of the spacious interior and ensur-ing that guests won't be left fumbling for the light switch. Old meets new, thus com-pleting the circle in a concept especially tailored to suit this unique location.

**A new take on a classic design – truly a
room for Berlin!**

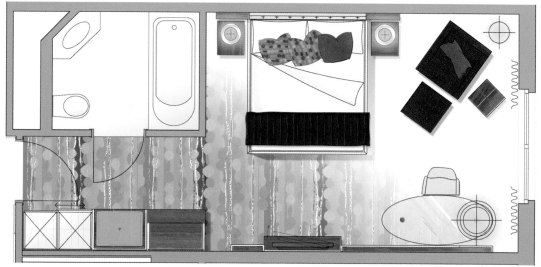

'Contemporary'
Guest Room Concept

Room Concept
Hotel Category: ★ ★ ★ ★
Hotel Type: Business hotel
The Brief: New construction / Designing a concept for a guest room
Floor area excl. bathrooms: 22.85 m²

A modern-day hotel room: calm and collected. The strength of this design is its attention to detail. The room layout is unlike most business hotel rooms: there is a walk-in closet, the dream of every business woman, with room for accessories and clothing for a variety of occasions, from lunch meetings to an evening gala. The future of hotels is feminine; after all, women are travelling more than ever before, especially for business.

The room is decorated in an elegant cream tone. In the centre of the room is the bed, framed and balanced by a high-gloss wall. Several shelves of varying sizes are set into the wall. Two niches form the bed stands, which appear as if folded out of the wall. Swivelling reading lights are flush to the wall and complete the ensemble. Besides the visual appeal of the design, the receded shelves store a variety of accessories for a female guest, from scarves to jewellery.

Stylish and practical – a hotel women will love.

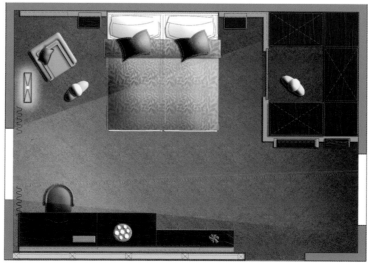

Cruiser
Cabin concept

Cabin Concept
Hotel Category: ★ ★ ★ ★ ★ superior
Hotel Type: Cruise ship
The Brief: Create a design concept for a cabin on the upper level of a new cruise ship
Floor area incl. bathrooms: 31.97 m²

You might think that a cruise ship is just a floating hotel, yet the design specifications are often far more complex. However, having said that, in this design concept we set out to create precisely that: a floating hotel room. Unlike most cabins on cruise ships, with built-in units along the walls to ensure nothing flies about in rough seas, this design truly has the style and feel of a luxurious hotel room!

Clear lines and a particular affinity for natural designs are the pillars of this concept. The cabin features a lavish external balcony, and is divided into a formal area and a more intimate sleeping area with ac-cess to the bathroom. A room divider with adjustable wooden slats ensures discretion while enhancing the flow of the room. Guests are likely to spend plenty of time in this cabin, and so the furniture has been carefully designed to ensure a high degree of flexibility, allowing guests to try out various combinations and personalize the layout of the room.

A floating hotel – a ship with all the comforts of life on shore.

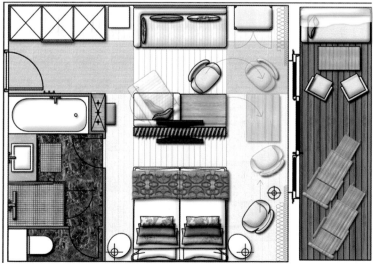

Crystal Tower
Berlin / Germany

Room Concept

Hotel Category: ★ ★ ★ ★ ★ superior

Hotel Type: City hotel

The Brief: New building / Produce a room design for a new luxury hotel

Floor area incl. bathrooms: 42.44 m²

Glittering like a crystal, this hotel makes a bold statement. Its irregular crystalline form echoes the diversity of this bustling metropolis, while setting the tone for the design. A clever facelift transforms the bathroom into an integral design element: the diagonal lines soften the geometry of the floor plan and resemble the exterior surface of a crystal. The material: gold-frosted black glass. While the glass wall forms a partitioning element, its translucency and dynamic surface create a refined lighting effect, evoking an air of openness and freedom. The washbasins act as a sculptural partition within the bathroom,

while the layout of the individual elements breaks with more sterile designs to offer a generous and liberating sense of space. A chandelier positioned above the wash-basins shimmers softly through the glass wall, connecting the bathroom with the living area.

The soft textile materials form a visual contrast, underscoring the modern Grand Hotel character of this design and ensuring both a pleasant sensory experience and the necessary acoustic discretion.

A truly modern Grand Hotel featuring accomplished contemporary interpretations of classical elements.

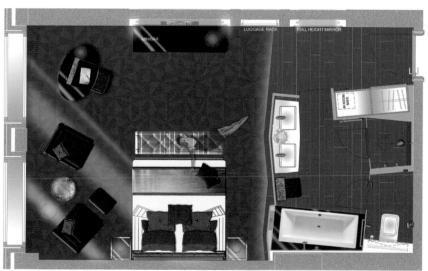

Crystal Tower
Berlin / Germany

Presidential Suite Concept
Hotel Category: ★ ★ ★ ★ superior
Hotel Type: City hotel
The Brief: New building / Design concept for the Presidential Suite
Floor area incl. bathrooms: 62.26 m²

Fittingly, the Presidential Suite is located on the penthouse level, with a stunning view of the Berlin city skyline, visible through the full-length window façade throughout the suite. The crystal shape of the design is delineated by the contours of three bathrooms and two stairwells. This form flows throughout the suite connecting the various areas with each other. Axes extend into the room like rays of light, and allow the space to be zoned into a public area with a guest room and a private area with a generous bathroom and sauna. For privacy, the zones can be completely separated. For a sense of spaciousness, the entire space can be left open.

Items of furniture and the hanging fireplace appear as individual sculptures in the distinctive structure of the room, adding a playful touch. The Presidential Suite offers ample space for a very special event, whether a business meeting or private dinner, with a panoramic view over the rooftops of Berlin.

A suite of possibilities: a brilliant gem that's above it all.

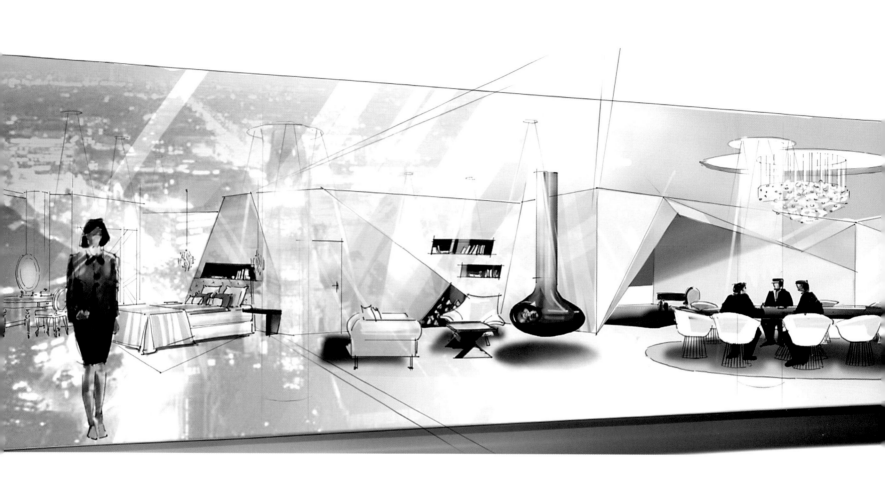

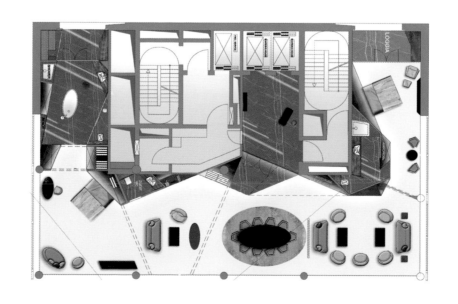

Dolce Hotel
Munich, Germany

Room Concept
Hotel Category: ★ ★ ★ ★
Hotel Type: Conference hotel
The Brief: New building /
Create a design concept for a room
Floor area incl. bathrooms: 26.74 m²

This conference hotel close to Munich airport has a distinctly Bavarian flavour. The public areas set the mood with their light-hearted take on the occasionally quirky culture of southern Germany – a welcome distraction from conference events and a very personal approach to engaging with guests. Opparated by an American hotel chain, the individual style of the design sets this hotel apart from its peers.
The rooms themselves are more reserved and offer guests a quiet environment to unwind after completing their business. The interior layout reflects contemporary demands for functionality and style with a

large business desk forming a free-standing design element. The bathroom design is spacious and features a walk-in shower and separate toilet. And for those who like to take a breather while they shower, there is even a bench! A window connects the bathroom and sleeping area, with a stylish etching ensuring the necessary degree of privacy. Natural materials ensure an even flow between the private and public areas.

Bavaria meets business – a place to unwind.

Dolce Hotel
Munich, Germany

Presidential Suite Concept
Hotel Category: ★ ★ ★ ★
Hotel Type: Conference hotel
The Brief: New building / Create a design concept for the presidential suite
Floor area incl. bathrooms: 74.60 m²

Located on the top floor and commanding an excellent view of the surroundings, this suite is home to a very special attraction: a sauna with a spectacular view of the Alps! This spacious presidential suite has plenty of room to host meetings in an intimate atmosphere. Indeed, the suite is often booked for large conferences as it offers a place for smaller groups to meet in private as required. The suite is ideal for guests who need to concentrate on their work, and also provides a suitable location for a private dinner.

But it is the private sauna adjoining the bathroom with a window looking out onto the Alps that really steals the show! And rest assured – at this height nobody will be peeking! While many saunas tend to be rather cramped, the window offers an optimal solution to this problem, creating a spacious atmosphere and opening the room to a view that is simply unforgettable! A one-of-a-kind suite with a truly unique selling point.

High above Unterschleißheim: a sauna with a view to die for.

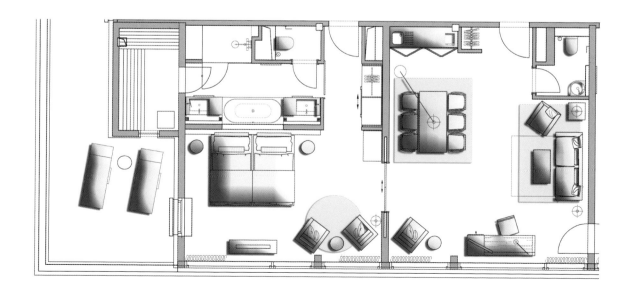

Dom Hotel
Cologne / Germany

Room Concept 'Next Generation'
Hotel Category: ★ ★ ★ ★ ★
Hotel Type: City hotel
The Brief: Complete refurbishment / Create a design concept for a room
Floor area incl. bathrooms: 30.00 m²

Designers are always trying to reinvent the hotel room – and in this case very successful: According to the teachings of Feng Shui, the curving walls of this interior design will enhance the flow of chi. A massage chair welcomes weary guests into its relaxing embrace at the end of their day. A shower screen of "shattered" safety glass breaks the line of the wall and floods the bathroom with light, while its crystalline structure ensures privacy.

A projector above the bed casts dreamscapes onto the ceiling above the bed: everything from sheep jumping over a fence, to underwater worlds, and the gently swaying canopy of a majestic forest.

The large walk-in wardrobe provides ample space for clothing and luggage. The bathroom is fashioned entirely from Corian, a material that is extremely pleasant to touch. Two islands of carpet mark off the living and sleeping areas. The "real" desk offers guests a place to prepare or review their day's work, while its inconspicuous style gives centre stage to the bed and massage chair.

A new way of thinking about hotel rooms.

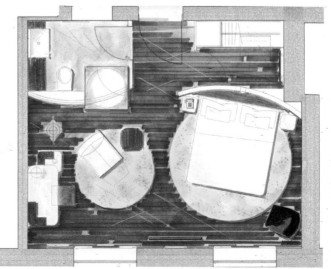

Dom Hotel
Cologne / Germany

Room Concept 'Blau-Gold Haus'
Hotel Category: ★ ★ ★ ★ ★ superior
Hotel Type: City hotel
The Brief: New building /
Extension for new guest rooms:
Create a design concept for a room
Floor area incl. bathrooms: 38.04 m²

This unique hotel is situated on Cologne's magnificent Cathedral Square. Facing the front entrance of the world-famous cathedral, the hotel occupies a listed historic building from the 1950s. Its stunning exterior is matched by the equally luxurious interior design.

The golden fluting of the building's façade is revisited on the headboard, the lighting fixtures are strictly 1950s, and the wardrobe is mounted on feet and features glass doors. But this is certainly not just another study in retro design – this hotel is not afraid to leave classical role models by the wayside and showcase its own unique architectural vision.

Finely veneered walnut, gold, velvet and leather furnishings and fixtures make for a distinctive look. The colour scheme is elegant, reserved, and subdued.

The rooms are spacious to the point of over-indulgence. The bathroom is simply huge, and features a bath tub, shower, and separate toilet. The room is furnished with a chaise longue and other pieces of furniture not usually found in a hotel room, such as a make-up table and a padded foot rest.

A luxury hotel in azure and gold: Upmarket elegance meets 1950s chic.

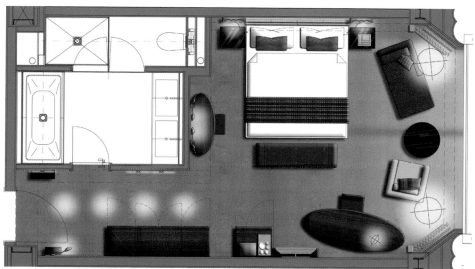

Doubletree by Hilton
Oradea / Romania

Room Concept

Hotel Category: ★ ★ ★ – ★ ★ ★ ★

Hotel Type: Conference hotel

The Brief: New building / Create a design concept for a room

Floor area incl. bathrooms: 31.59 m²

Situated in northwest Romania, Oradea is the site of an exciting project that will see the creation of a world-class international hotel with a local flavour.

Both the hotel operator and the designer recognised the need for a design that reflects the hotel's location – a guest travelling from New York, who spends one night in Rajastan and the next in Oradea, expects Western standards of comfort and service, and a design that communicates the flavour and style of the country they are visiting. The solution: a design with a neutral, international style and an eye-catching console, positioned facing the entrance, which depicts the historical fortified walls of Oradea.

The use of blue-tinted glazing in all of the windows renders warmer shades of yellow and red unpalatable, making it difficult to define a suitable colour scheme. Shades of brown and beige react well to these conditions, while blue and violet tones shine vividly in the filtered light. The neutral, cream colour scheme is set off by the blue-violet accents (armchair, cushions, bed runner).

An international design with a local focus.

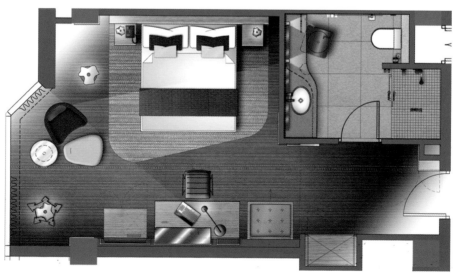

Dubai Pearl
Dubai / UAE

Suite Concept – Type E
Hotel Category: ★ ★ ★ ★ ★ superior
Hotel Type: City hotel
The Brief: New building / Create a design concept for a suite
Floor area incl. bathrooms: 68.89 m²

A special building for a special location: this design is intended for one of seven high-rise buildings planned as part of a new development in the heart of this exciting metropolis. Enjoying first-class views of the Palm Jumeirah project, the buildings are laid out in an elegant circle reminiscent of a pearl. Each of the buildings will fulfil a different function; this tower will house a luxury hotel.

This design for a premium suite located on the top floor of the hotel dazzles with its accomplished application of the organic motif throughout the interior. The soft curving forms shape the interior and fulfil a variety of functions. The first pearl in the floor marks off the reception area, while a second – decorated with an exquisite inlay – shields the private chambers and guides guests through to the bathroom and sleeping areas. The circular platform with its crescent-shaped sofa arrangement will seal the deal: this fully automated platform can be rotated through 360° to take in the suite's magnificent sea views!

The power of the pearl: a suite with push-button mobility.

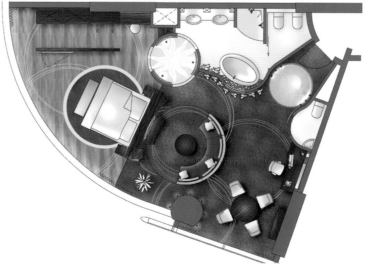

Suite Concept – Type D
Hotel Category: ★ ★ ★ ★ ★ superior
Hotel Type: City hotel
The Brief: New building / Create a
design concept for a suite
Floor area incl. bathrooms: 81.95 m²

This floor plan is for another luxury suite on the same level. Here, the continuous, full-length glazing offers guests unique and spectacular sea views.

Thanks to the suite's flexible design, guests can gaze out at the ocean from the sofa or catch up on the latest news and films on the flatscreen TV. As with the alternative design, this suite features a fully rotating platform that is easily adjusted to a variety of positions at the push of a button. This technology offers guests an optimal degree of communicative flexibility, allowing them to use the room both for private meetings and intimate dinners. The public area also includes a separate toilet for guests, and an eye-catching pearl inlay fashioned from glass mosaic tiles separates this area from the private rooms. The circular motif on the flooring around the bed accentuates its stylish design, while the bathroom is accessible via a handsome walk-in wardrobe.

The sign of the pearl – putting a new twist on excellence.

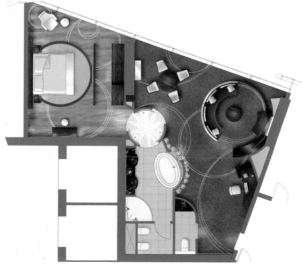

Extended stay Apartments
Frankfurt Main / Germany

Room Concept
Hotel Category: ★ ★ ★ ★
Hotel Type: City hotel
The Brief: Complete renovation /
Designing a concept for a guest room
Floor area incl. bathrooms: 32.57 m²

Whether by doctors or lawyers – for research, advanced studies, or a seminar – reasons abound for a longer stay in Frankfurt am Main. These rooms are suited for the extended guest, and include a full pantry service. The bed and armchair are located in the quieter area in front of the window, a perfect place to relax and read or kick back after work is done. The bookshelf underneath the window has space to leave books after they've been read, and offers used books others have left behind. Throughout the room there is ample storage and table space for all the things extended stay guests brings with them.

Located in the centre of the room is a multifunctional table, which accommodates breakfast just as well as it does a laptop. It frames the room, shields the quiet zone in the back, and ties the entire design together. Built-in drawers hold all kinds of knickknacks and necessities, from pens to pictures of loved ones.

Extended stay in style – a room you can personalise.

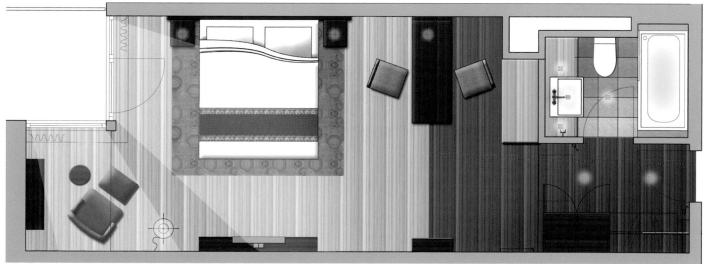

Fibonacci Hotel
Prague / Czech Republic

Room concept
Hotel Category: ★ ★ ★ – ★ ★ ★ ★
Hotel Type: City hotel
The Brief: Conversion of an existing building into a hotel / Development of a design concept for a guest room
Floor area incl. bathrooms: 18.96 m²

In the midst of numerous new hotels in Prague, this design concept stands out. The focus is on 'sustainability', with models drawn from the natural world. The ancient substance of the building, a grand city residence, is enlivened and transformed in a natural manner. Irregular shapes and asymmetric proportions attract attention, while the unique spatial arrangement makes more of the limited floor space; the bed is positioned in the quietest zone, with the recliner and desk in front. The bath is enclosed by a semi-transparent, back-lit curtain in a wide arc. A suitcase stand and wardrobe are hidden behind the curtain, as is the bathroom,

adding a second layer of privacy to this most private of spots. The translucent quality of the back-lit curtain adds a sense of depth to the room. Upon entering, we find a small bookcase instead of a television screen, which is positioned subtly in the far corner. The room is set in natural hues, predominantly a soft green, bright natural tones, and greys. Keeping with the focus on sustainability, materials such as solid wood, felt, and wool are essential here, as are living plants, while the floral motif is picked up in fabrics and wall coverings.

Fibonacci – Design inspired by nature.

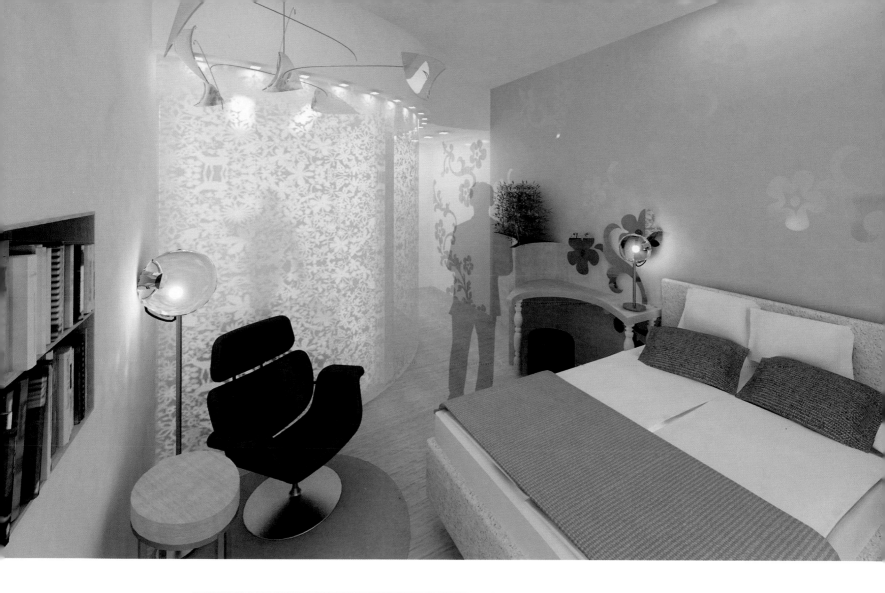

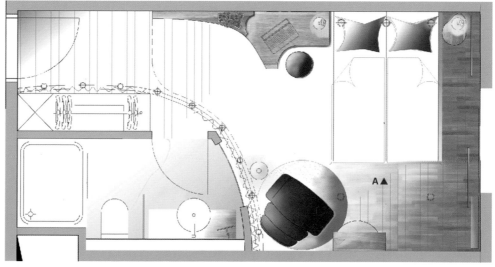

Fibonacci Hotel
Prague / Czech Republic

Twin Bed Room Concept
Hotel Category: ★ ★ ★ – ★ ★ ★ ★
Hotel Type: City hotel
The Brief: Conversion of an existing building into a hotel / Develop a design concept for a twin bed room
Floor area incl. bathrooms: 21.86 m^2

With its spacious foyer and organic forms, this corner room offers guests a warm welcome. The gentle curve of the parquet flooring as it meets the carpeting in the living area carries over into the design of the desk. Echoing the contour of the corner of the building, this sculptural element marks the transition to the sleeping and living areas, where the design opens to explore the vertical dimension.

Building on this clever use of form, the swirling patterns on the wall panelling emphasise the elevated ceiling and draw on the Art Nouveau architecture of this historical town house. The snail-like form of the desk is connected to the adjoining wall by its upstand, forming a continuum with the outer shell of the room.

The materials and colours follow the same principle and feature delicate natural floral patterns. The headboard on the bed is crafted from a tree root and accentuates the stylised legs of the bedside tables – an exciting contrast of natural design elements and the urban elegance of a true city hotel.

Nature is the prototype: a design grounded in location.

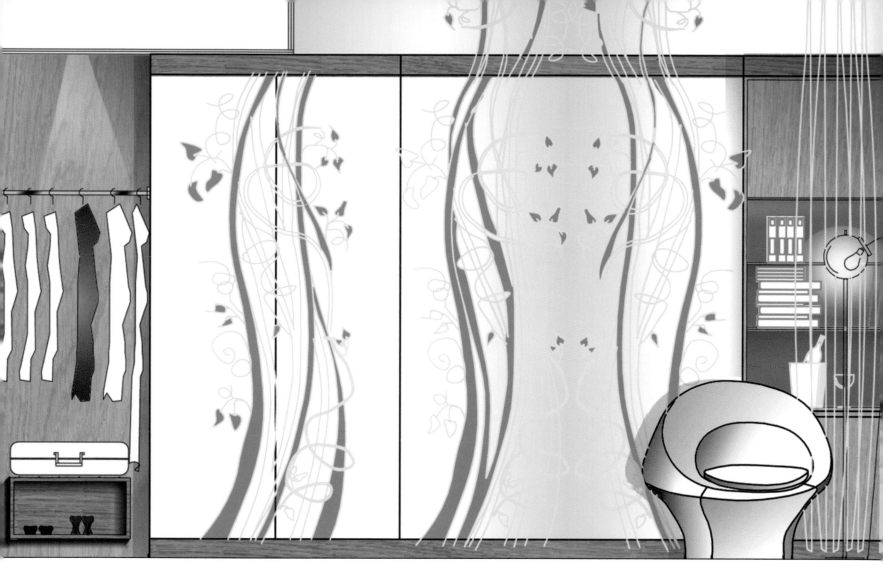

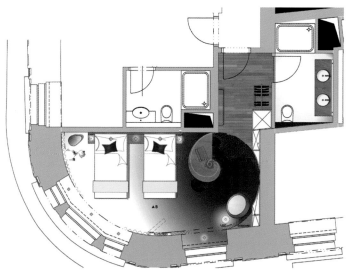

Fitness Hotel
Hamburg / Germany

Room Concept
Hotel Category: ★ ★ ★ ★
Hotel Type: Sport and wellness hotel
The Brief: New building / Create a design concept for a room
Floor area incl. bathrooms: 31.24 m²

Situated at a prominent location in Hamburg, this new hotel features an integrated fitness centre and spa, complemented by a room design that puts guests in the right mindset for working out and provides a place to unwind.

Together with the Stadtpark – the city's green lung – the twin basins of the Inner and Outer Alster make Hamburg a verdant metropolis. The room design makes the most of this, infusing the room with a lush aura of health and vitality.

The open layout of the floor plan offers guests an unimpeded view through to the façade as they enter the room. The bath-room opens onto and connects the entrance and sleeping areas, with the shower forming a monolithic block between the two. The bathroom opens up the floor plan, creating a spacious feel. This impression is strengthened by its exterior; a subtle reinterpretation of conventional forms that lends the wall the appearance of a decorative partition screen. The blend of natural colours and organic motifs is complemented by the urban motif above the bed.

An oasis in the city – a young and refreshing design blend with a feel for nature.

Fleethotel
Hamburg / Germany

Concept Suites

Hotel Category: ★ ★ ★ ★ ★ superior

Hotel Type: City hotel

The Brief: Total refurbishment / Create a design concept for a suite

Floor area incl. bathrooms: 58.08 m²

This versatile design will astonish guests! A formal business suite suitable for meeting and entertaining clients and partners, this suite is easily transformed into an open-plan wellness suite with a truly stunning bathroom.

Sliding doors enable guests to separate and join various parts of the suite as they please. The bathroom can be closed off while allowing visitors to the suite access to the toilet. Alternatively, guests can link the toilet and bathroom for private use. Other highlights include a "snail shell shower" (allowing for an open-plan shower design), a free-standing spa pool, a dual-access toilet, a lockable walk-in wardrobe, a vanity/work unit in the bedroom, and a living/dining area which also serves as a conference room.

In keeping with the multifunctional design, the colour scheme features subdued, dark, masculine tones appropriate to a business setting, while wood shades and cream-coloured walls communicate a warm elegance – all that guests have to is throw open the doors to transform their spacious bathroom into a private spa centre!

A luxurious business suite for discerning guests in the heart of Hamburg.

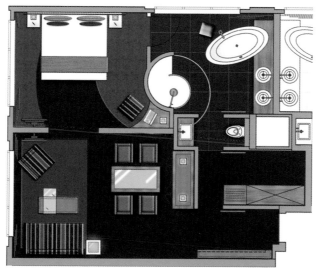

'Future Visions'
Guest Room Concept

Room Concept
Hotel Category: ★ ★ ★ ★ ★
Hotel Type: Airport hotel
The Brief: New building / Create a design concept for a room
Floor area incl. bathrooms: 30.35 m²

Situated in close proximity to the airport, this hotel sports a decidedly aerodynamic design that plays with a range of dynamic forms adopted from the building's exterior. The floating style of the furniture is perfectly matched to the location, underscoring the finesse of a design in which flow and comfort are the key factors. The warm colour scheme balances the hi-tech flair, creating a soothing atmosphere for weary travellers.

The direct line of sight from the entrance to the armchair subtly reinforces this effect. This is a place where you can flop down and let your thoughts wander. The round forms have a calming effect, forming a natural counterpoint to the hustle and bustle of metropolitan life.

The sweeping curve of the spacious four-piece bathroom features a number of lighting slits, linking the bathroom with the living area. This dynamic form is reflected in the elliptic installation on the wall opposite: a multifunctional wardrobe, desk, bench and suitcase rack. A similar figure decorates the floor where it forms a natural catwalk and rounds off the design.

Floating furniture and playful curves.

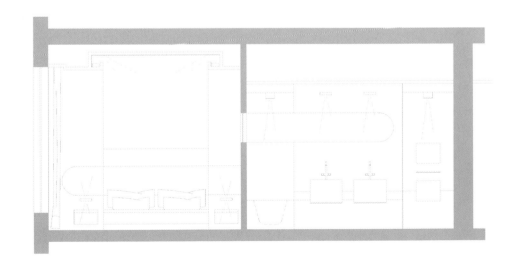

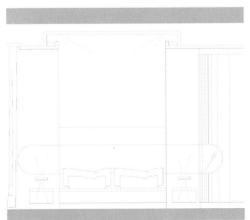

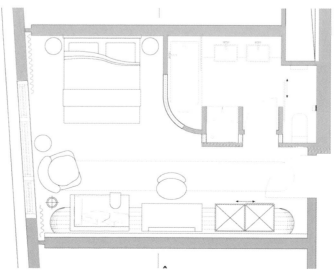

Hotel Gendarm nouveau
Berlin / Germany

Room Concept
Hotel Category: ★ ★ ★ ★
Hotel Type: City hotel
The Brief: Complete refurbishment /
Create a design concept for a room
Floor area incl. bathrooms: 26.25 m²

A cultural hotspot: the opulent architecture of Berlin's Gendarmenmarkt sets the tone for this design. Experience history in a design that combines timeless elegance with the clear lines of modern furnishings. Classic accents in the here and now: glossy accent colours set off the classic style of the turned table legs. Custom lighting fixtures reflect the beauty of the turned table legs, while the flatscreen TV nestles in a contoured frame adorning the wall. Guests will feel as though they are visiting friends, an impression that is reinforced by the unconventional details: the bedside tables are adorned with framed images reminiscent of Friedrich Schiller's poetry and the beauty of the ensemble of Französischer Dom and Deutscher Dom, which are just a few steps away. The customised design concept is visible throughout the building – history can be felt in every corner. The composition is completed by the lighting – a distinctive blend of traditional and Modernist style that was purpose-built for the hotel.

History in a contemporary design with delightfully playful details.

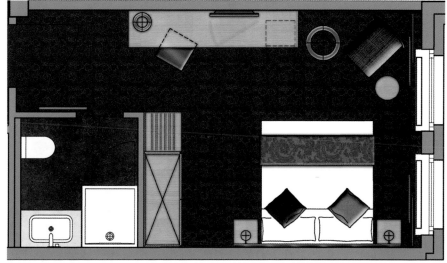

Hotel Gendarm nouveau
Berlin / Germany

SPA Suite Concept
Hotel Category: ★ ★ ★ ★
Hotel Type: City hotel
The Brief: Complete refurbishment /
Create a design concept for the SPA suite
Floor area incl. bathrooms: 28.95 m²

This is a suite for tourists and business guests alike – situated on the top floor, this spacious suite commands an impressive view of Berlin's Gendarmenmarkt and has a warm atmosphere that will welcome guests into its embrace at the end of their day. The massive sloping rooftop windows look out on the square below, which is flanked by the Französischer Dom and Deutscher Dom towers and the Konzerthaus, while a monument in the centre of the square commemorates the life of the German poet Friedrich Schiller. Guests will revel in the rich historical legacy of this site.

The show-stopper: the bath tub is positioned in the centre of the room facing the panoramic windows, allowing guests to gaze out across this magnificent city while they relax in a steaming bath. The free-standing bath is positioned on a tiled island that flows across the room like a gentle wave, drawing the room together and connecting the various elements in a design that marries functionality with an accomplished aesthetic sensibility.

Enjoy a slice of history: a suite with a view.

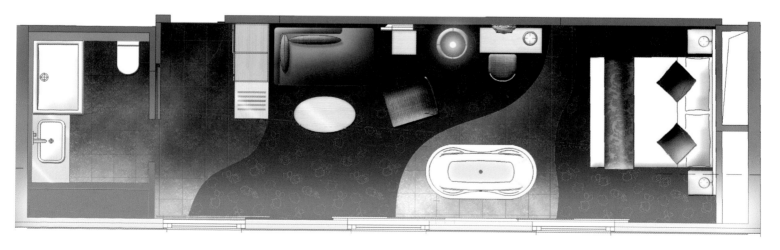

Hotel Gendarm nouveau
Berlin / Germany

Room Concept
Hotel Category: ★ ★ ★ ★
Hotel Type: City hotel
The Brief: Total refurbishment /
Conversion of existing office rooms into
additional hotel rooms: Create a
design concept for a guest room
Floor area incl. bathrooms: 26.82 m²

With the addition of the Gendarm Suites, which were added to the building at a later date, Hotel Gendarm Nouveau's portfolio grew to a total of 42 rooms and suites. The new business floor is particularly luxurious and has a more masculine flavour.
A hotel room styled like a business suit: black, anthracite – complemented by vibrant rosewood textures. The sophisticated style of the rooms is underscored by the use of cutting-edge lighting techniques. The oval desk is large and spacious – just as it should be in a business room. In fact, the desk is large enough to fit two comfortable desk chairs! Equipped with a host of

discretely integrated plugs and ports, its design makes the desk seem more like a private bureau or a side table – nobody needs a constant reminder of work in their room. A second oval form fits neatly under the shelf that extends along the wall: yet another plush armchair. The crescent-shaped bay in the sideboard guides the armchair back to its original position.

A stylish business suite in black – a tailor-made design.

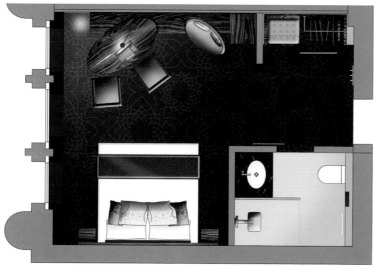

Golden Arch Hotel
Zurich, Switzerland

Room Concept
Hotel Category: ★ ★ ★ ★
Hotel Type: Airport hotel
The Brief: New building /
Create a design concept for a room
Floor area incl. bathrooms: 24.88 m²

Backed by its American big sister, this hotel, which opened near Zurich airport, marks a world first: the fast food chain's first venture into the hotel industry.
In a bold move that breaks with conventions the open design of the bathroom features a centrally positioned cylindrical shower stall.
Seizing the opportunity presented by this unique joint venture the design questions conventional solutions and translates tradition into a contemporary style. The outcome is refreshingly different: the rippling curve of the partitioning wall extends the floor plan into the adjacent room. The resulting alcove houses a desk, and the revolving column beside it is home to a state-of-the-art infotainment system, so guests can surf the Internet from the comfort of their bed. The beds are equipped with comfort controls that enable guests to individually adjust the back and foot rests. And the colour scheme? The parent company's signature colours are accompanied by a range of natural tones, light parquet flooring, and a shade of green that complements the sweeping curve of the crimson red wall.
Experience another side of the golden arches.

Golf Resort
Belek / Turkey

Room Concept

Hotel Category: ★ ★ ★ ★ ★ superior

Hotel Type: Luxury resort

The Brief: New Building / Create a design for a deluxe room at a new hotel complex with an adjoining golf course

Floor area incl. bathrooms: 52.94 m²

Different countries, different customs: this design welcomes guests with a lavish foyer and bathroom. With its generous seating area and numerous cushions, the adjoining living area has a distinctively Turkish flair. The fabric canopy above the bed creates a cosy, protective atmosphere, while referencing traditional Turkish décor. Pendulum lamps fitted with elegant lampshades set off the scene and lend the sleeping area a light, buoyant style. Translucent mashrabiyas round off the play of historical and contemporary styles, framing the elongated seating niche and artfully integrating this cosy haven. Tiled flooring is widespread in South East European domiciles, and while it's an unusual element in a hotel, it's so much more hygienic here! The elaborate patterns of the rugs adorning the tiled floors are revisited in the seating area. In the centre of the bathroom a decorative floor inlay fashioned from exquisite mosaic tiles forms an eye-catching feature. His-and-hers washbasins and a separate toilet create an aura of luxury and abundance. A walk-in wardrobe opposite the bathroom is discretely concealed using intelligently designed folding elements.

A luxury resort straight from The Arabian Nights – an accomplished blend of tradition and modernism.

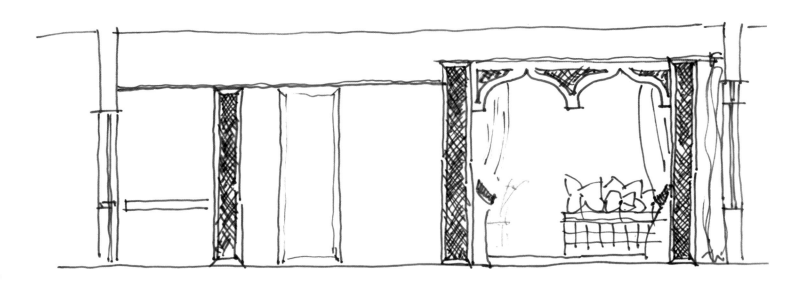

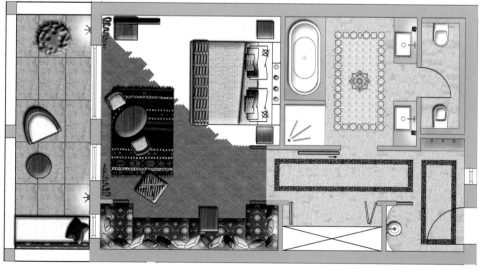

Golf Resort
Belek / Turkey

Townhouse Concept
Hotel Category: ★ ★ ★ ★ ★ superior
Hotel Type: Luxury resort
The Brief: New building / Design concept
for a townhouse at a new hotel complex
with an adjoining golf course
Floor area incl. bathrooms: 84.51 m²

This townhouse with cooking facilities lends a touch of luxury to a golfing holiday with the family. Some larger units even have enough room to accommodate two families. Guests have the option of cooking for themselves in the spacious kitchen or of dining out in one of the resort's restaurants.

The building is designed around the external patio, which is centrally located and visible through the large panorama window in the living area. This is far more than an access point to fresh air; rather, it is the key living space within the building. For an even greater sense of spaciousness, the panorama window can be opened completely.

Ottoman stylistic elements are featured throughout the townhouse in fabrics and patterns. These are traditional yet suited to modern sensibilities. The living area is of paramount importance in this concept, as it has always been in Turkish culture. It is not without reason that terms such as "ottoman" and "divan" come from Turkish, reflecting the importance that the Turks attribute to the home.

An oasis of comfort and luxury for more discerning holidaymakers: a place to replenish the spirit.

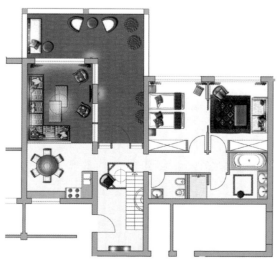

Grand Hotel
Vienna / Austria

Junior Suite Concept
Hotel Category: ★ ★ ★ ★ ★ superior
Hotel Type: City hotel
The Brief: Complete refurbishment /
Create a design concept for a junior suite
Floor area incl. bathrooms: 56.13 m²

Tradition revisited: taking its cue from the Hofburg and Schönbrunn palaces, this design captures the essence of Viennese style at the height of the Imperial Age. While other hotels reinterpret past designs, authenticity is the non-plus-ultra here. The result is a painstakingly detailed design that recreates the accomplished style of the Viennese court without resorting to papier-mâché or props: everything is real, everything is authentic. Welcome to the Age of Splendour!

Taking spaciousness to new heights: the elevated ceilings will take your breath away! There is plenty of room for guests to let their thoughts wander – the generous floor plan gives the exquisite furnishings the space they need to look their best. Guests can unwind at the end of a long day on the suite's sumptuous chaise longue or relax in the wing chair. But the highlight of this suite must be the bed: its stunning upholstered headboard and elaborate drapery will transport guests into an age long past – the perfect ending to a busy day in the Imperial City.

A suite worthy of the Habsburgs – experience Viennese luxury up close.

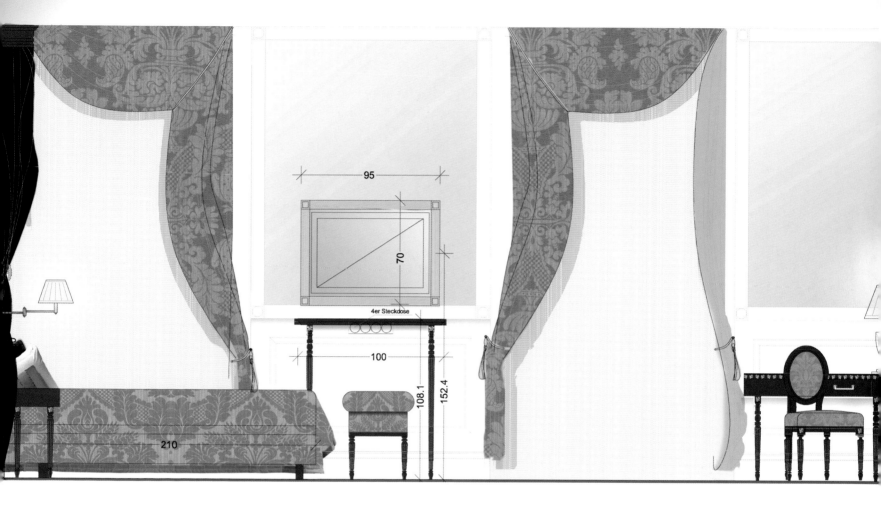

95

70

4er Steckdose

100

108.1

152.4

210

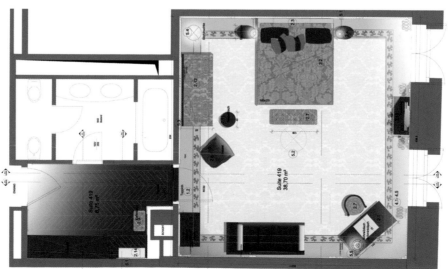

Grand Hotel
Vienna / Austria

Superior Room Concept
Hotel Category: ★ ★ ★ ★ ★ superior
Hotel Type: City hotel
The Brief: Complete refurbishment / Create a design concept for a superior room
Floor area incl. bathrooms: 29.23 m²

Vienna – the very name conjures up images of horse-drawn carriages and Sacher Torte, the glorious Schönbrunn and Hofburg palaces, and the story of Princess Sissi. History has been kept alive at the Grand Hotel on Vienna's Ringstrasse, and the atmosphere of this legendary hotel next to the State Opera is charged with all the pomp and circumstance of a royal court.

The high ceilings give the rooms a palatial flair, while the furnishings evoke memories of the Imperial Age: individual pieces are carefully positioned about the room like antiques, elaborate drapery frames the view of the thoroughfare below, and the impressive stucco adorning the walls complements the exquisite fabric wall coverings. Gilded elements and elaborate trimmings add depth to this artistic vision, creating a unique room in which the past and present enter into a breathtaking dialogue. A fitting design for a hotel room in this imperial city on the Danube and a testament to Vienna's glorious past. An authentic experience: history you can feel!

Viennese style: a room with a history!

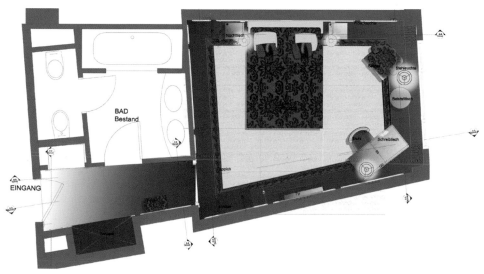

Green Hotel
Prague / Czech Republic

Room Concept
Hotel Category: ★ ★ ★ – ★ ★ ★ ★
Hotel Type: City hotel
The Brief: New building / Designing a concept for a guest room
Floor area incl. bathrooms: 24.28 m²

Nature compels us to see the future with new eyes. This modular room design proposes a responsible approach to resource consumption; a hotel room, after all, provides multiple ways to consume or conserve resources: light and water, heat and cold. When multiplied by all the rooms of a hotel, the potential for savings becomes considerable.

By focusing on nature, the design reminds us that our consumption of resources directly depends on our behaviour. Each room is designed around nature at its most stunning, climaxing in the wall coverings over the bed and onto the ceiling, each one featuring large-scale images from nature. A sense of protection, a sense of security radiates from these visions of the natural world, which vary from floor to floor. Green is the essential colour and theme of the hotel, as reflected in renewable materials for furnishings and energy-saving fixtures in the rooms. Perhaps all this beauty is capable of opening a few eyes to a more conscious approach to energy consumption.

For the love of nature – a room with a social message.

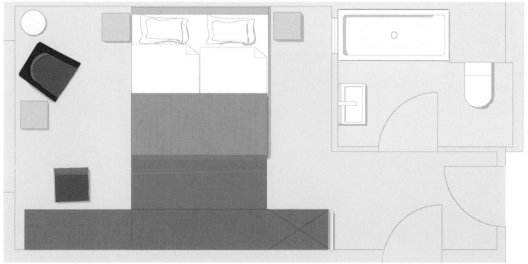

'Green Room'
Guest Room Concept

Room Concept
Hotel Category: ★ ★ ★ ★
Hotel Type: City hotel
The Brief: New building / Create a design concept for a room
Floor area excl. bathrooms: 23.98 m²

Sustainability is all about forward-looking concepts. And while sustainable design is a topical issue, it has yet to make its mark in many hotels. This room design truly embraces sustainability.

The unusual layout of the floor plan reflects the room's integration within the larger complex – the images showcase the living and sleeping area, but not the bathroom. The eye-catcher here is a green lung: while this wall of living greenery requires a lot of attention, it lends the interior a unique and refreshing atmosphere. The wooden desk positioned against the wall features a multifunctional design and doubles as a make-up table with bark details on the legs adding an organic touch. The natural wooden flooring is decorated with an inlay and a felt rug, while the translucent fabric canopy above the centrally positioned bed transforms it into an oasis of tranquillity. A seating island rounds off the concept and features a curvaceous, solid wood armchair beneath a light installation that conjures up visions of softly floating bubbles under water. Quite simply, this room is an homage to nature!

The future is green – possibly the first sustainable hotel room.

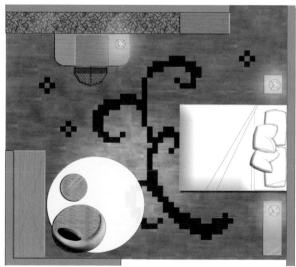

Hilton Hotel Danube
Vienna / Austria

Room Concept
Hotel Category: ★ ★ ★ ★ ★
Hotel Type: Conference hotel
The Brief: Complete refurbishment /
Create a design concept for a room
Floor area incl. bathrooms: 38.41 m²

A unique location on the banks of the Danube. Relax and let your eyes wander across the spectacular view of the Danube from this elegant hotel. The river itself was the source of inspiration for this interior design. Conference guests will appreciate the quiet seclusion of the hotel – an ideal location for focussed meetings, far from the hubbub of the big city, but close to the trade fair centre and airport. The hotel is located on the periphery of the city, and is easily accessible. This is a place to meet colleagues, learn, listen, debate, and find new inspiration. The gently flowing river will sooth nerves and focus minds.

The Danube has also left its mark on the room design: black, cream, and dark red dominate the colour scheme. Gentle waves wash across the headboard and drapes, the tables rest like pebbles on a riverbed, while floral motifs complement the elegant black and white look: the strict Art Nouveau style of the Vienna Secession art movement rounds off the composition and roots this design in its location.

Viennese elegance on the banks of the Danube.

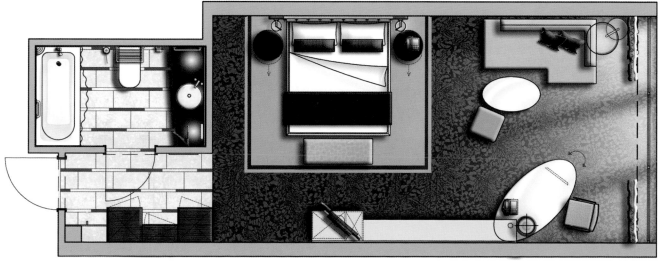

Hilton Hotel
Frankfurt-Airport / Germany

Room Concept

Hotel Category: ★ ★ ★ ★ ★

Hotel Type: Airport hotel

The Brief: New building / Designing a concept for a guest room

Floor area incl. bathrooms: 30.30 m²

The project is located in direct proximity to Frankfurt International Airport, in an unusual cigar-shaped structure on stilts. The long-distance train station is directly below, and the building complex also enjoys immediate access to the autobahn. The airport terminals are in walking distance. In terms of dimensions, the building is twice as long as the Empire State Building is high – and a full third of this length is dedicated to the Hilton family: the Hilton Hotel and the Hilton Garden Inn. Together, they offer nearly 600 rooms, an impressive response to the enormous stream of visitors.

The interior exudes a sense of calm, as passengers-cum-guests to this Hilton are looking for a respite from jet fumes, high-decibel engines and stress. Upon entering the room, guests are met by an updated version of the classic wing chair, underscoring the casual elegance of the room. The art concept is unique to this project, uniting technology and nature. The modern structure is left exposed, while a wave-patterned carpet and selected wooden surfaces are given a prominent focus.

A landmark project: mobility and progress combined with understated elegance.

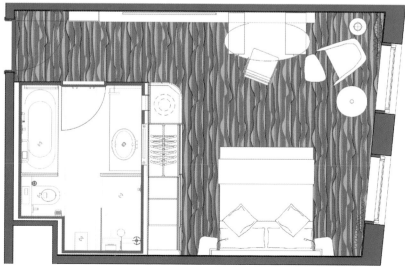

Hilton Hotel
Frankfurt-Airport / Germany

Presidential Suite Concept
Hotel Category: ★ ★ ★ ★ ★
Hotel Type: Airport hotel
The Brief: New building / Design concept for the Presidential Suite
Floor area incl. bathrooms: 162.40 m²

Within walking distance of one of the world's busiest airports is a fantastic view of the mountains: from the top of the futuristic building in Frankfurt you can see the Taunus mountain range. Time to relax, time to land for a spell. The hubbub of travel seems far away, and the next appointment can wait. Up here, a quiet view is an exceptional luxury after the crowds at the gate.

Floral patterns and high-quality materials, classic furniture and just a hint of gold – perhaps more than just a hint. The Presidential Suite is a cut above the other rooms, and exudes an exceptional feel-

ing of comfort, discretion, and esteem. The public area with a large living room and conference / private dining room has its own entrance, as does the pantry: the staff and deliveries do not disturb the guests here. Further along, the sleeping area features a jacuzzi in the centre, and a spacious dressing area. This is luxury for discriminating guests: a room that leaves little to be desired.

Saving the best for last: a distinctive suite.

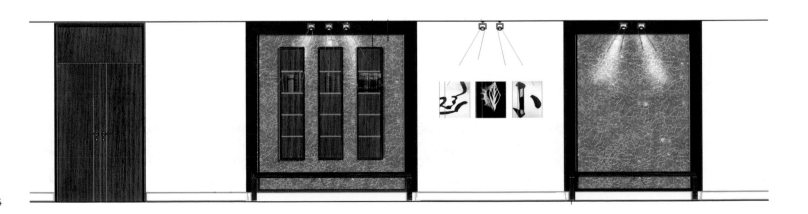

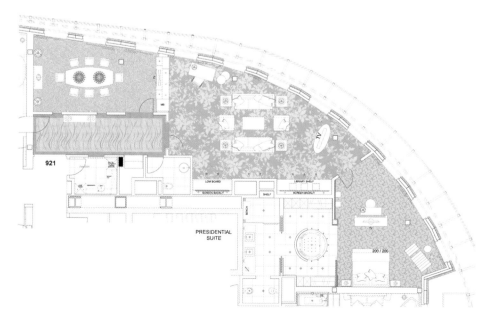

PRESIDENTIAL SUITE

Holiday village
Mecklenburg Lake District / Germany

Room Concept
Hotel Category: ★ ★ ★ ★
Hotel Type: Holiday lodges
The Brief: New building / Designing a concept for a guest room
Floor area incl. bathrooms: 28.80 m²

With a barbecue and playground at its doorstep and a restaurant and disco on site, this lakeside holiday cottage is nestled in a landscape of lush greenery. It's the perfect place for young families to take a break and unwind. Rather than opting for a central hotel complex, the architect created a veritable holiday village by scattering small cottages about the site – all the interior designers had to do was take that casual holiday atmosphere indoors. The small timber-framed cottages set clear constraints, but allow for a bright, contemporary, and family-friendly design. The solution is a congenial blend of histori-cal fachwerk elements and contemporary zeitgeist. The white laminated flooring adds a stylish accent and ensures that guests experience the cottage as a wholly contemporary space. The yellow sofa adds a splash of sunshine, while the furnishings, pictures, and fabrics draw on natural motifs. The abstract foliage adorning the lamp above the table combines with the driftwood bedside lamps to underscore the hotel's natural setting.

Modern family living in a natural environment.

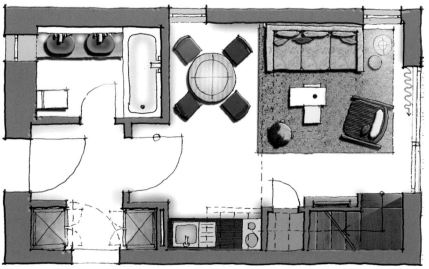

Hotel am Zwinger
Dresden / Germany

Room Concept
Hotel Category: ★ ★ ★ ★
Hotel Type: Conference hotel
The Brief: New building / Create a design concept for a room
Floor area incl. bathrooms: 23.79 m²

History abounds in Dresden: this proud metropolis is full of monuments to the past, and a new hotel cannot afford to ignore them. Visitors to the city want to stay at a hotel that has a clear yet contemporary relationship to the historic locale – a hotel that takes a frank and open approach to the history of this world-famous city without appearing stern or stuffy. Guests want to live and breathe history without being burdened by it. They want to see the modern Dresden and understand how the city has come to terms with its past.
This room design is all about creating clear lines and open spaces: the room breaks with conventional designs which position the bed in the niche created by closing off the bathroom. Instead, the bed is positioned in the centre of the room with a view towards the window. The bathroom, meanwhile, opens onto the living area, enhancing the flow and creating a spacious look.

A young design for modern Dresden.

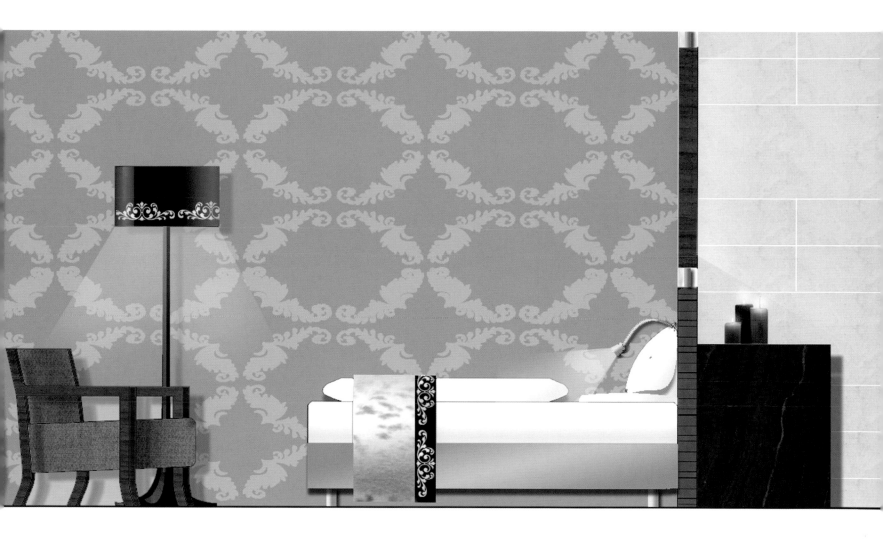

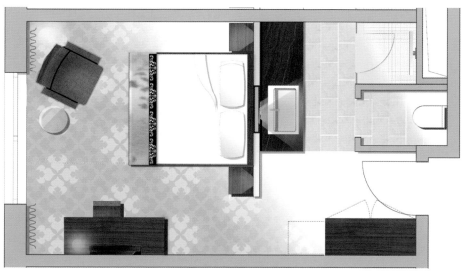

Hotel an der Musikhalle
Hamburg / Germany

Room Concept
Hotel Category: ★ ★ ★ ★
Hotel Type: City hotel
The Brief: New building / Create a design concept for a room
Floor area incl. bathrooms: 24.63 m²

This modern building is located adjacent to the Musikhalle, Hamburg's famous concert hall: music and architecture – a fusion of rhythms, movement, and harmony. Classical music meets modern architecture as a young hospitality product engages with tradition. Elements from both worlds come together to create a forward-looking design that is firmly rooted in its distinctive location. This hotel will receive a wide range of guests – from concert-goers to shopaholics, tourists, conference participants and business guests. This is a hotel for all occasions: a modern hotel for a modern city. The design contrasts contemporary furnishings with classic pieces in an inspiring dialogue that is reminiscent of a musical masterpiece as it explores the full potential of its themes to create something fresh, new, and dynamic. Across the room, a capitone headboard adds a tranquil note to the design – this memory of times past is complemented by an eye-catching chandelier that is visible through the window to the shower. The armchair rests on a verdant green island of peace – a place to rest your legs between appointments.

Hamburg calling – a meeting of classic and modern styles.

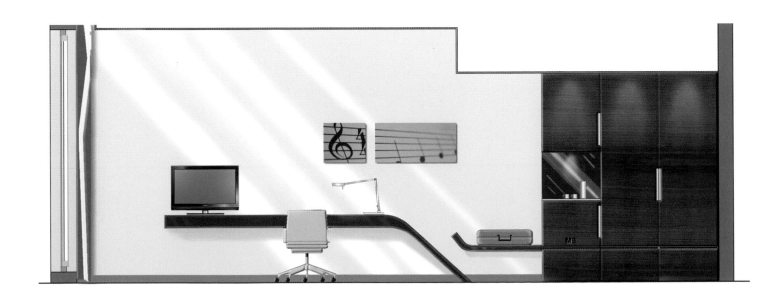

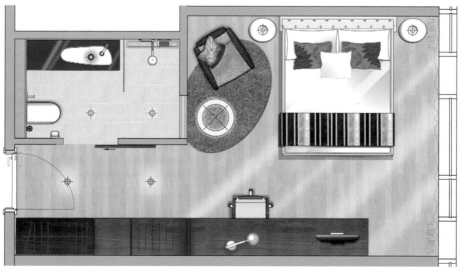

Hotel di Arte e Cultura
Tuscany, Italy

Room Concept
Hotel Category: ★ ★ ★ ★ superior
Hotel Type: Resort hotel
The Brief: New building /
Create a design concept for a room
Floor area incl. bathrooms: 27.80 m²

Balsam for the soul: an oasis of tranquillity deep in the mountains of Tuscany. This is a resort for the discerning traveller with a taste for the arts and culture. Holidaymakers staying here will want to explore the customs and traditions of Tuscany rather than spend their days at the beach. This is a place where guests can relax and immerse themselves in another culture. Here they can find out how olive oil and wine are produced, and how to make a proper cappuccino. Welcome to a hotel for holidaymakers who want to find out what goes on behind the scenes! Traditional motifs feature throughout the rooms and combine with a dollop of good

humour to create an ensemble that will inspire guests. For example, though the Madonna is normally found at roadside shrines or on the corners of public buildings, a modern interpretation hangs above the bed ready to bless weary travellers. This artistic design features clear lines with a southern European flair: the furnishings and lighting have a sculptural quality that sets off the room.

Discover la dolce vita: a room for explorers.

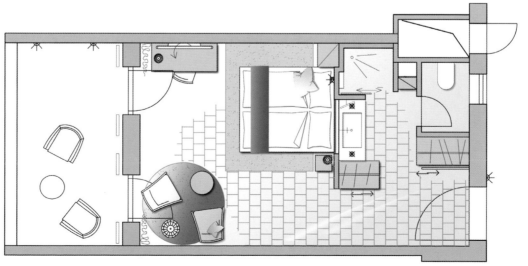

Hotel Klee
Berlin, Germany

Room Concept
Hotel Category: ★ ★ ★ ★ superior
Hotel Type: City hotel
The Brief: Complete refurbishment /
Create a design concept for a room
Floor area incl. bathrooms: 19.80 m²

A design inspired by art: a painting by Paul Klee provided the inspiration for the furnishings, colours, and structure of this interior design. Layers, shifts, contrasts, scales, and colour are combined in a room that will revitalize guests like no other. How do we live history? How do we experience images? The answer to both of these questions lies in a combination of order and motion. Blue represents sleep, life, and the bright sky of day. Orange stands for twilight: a time of rest. These colours are inspiring, soothing, and stimulating at once – order and motion. The design draws the colours, surfaces, and proportions of Klee's masterpiece together in a new vision: the result is a thematic cluster of furnishings, textiles, and lighting elements. The harmonious colour scheme and carefully balanced proportions have a soothing effect: guests will instantly feel at ease in this room. The building's elevated ceiling gives the composition plenty of space to breathe, enabling the design to reach its full potential.

A room, a painting – a masterpiece revisited.

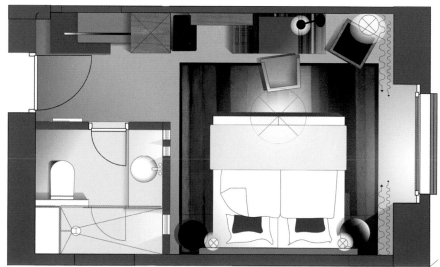

Jagdschloss
Spreewald / Germany

Room Concept
Hotel Category: ★ ★ ★ ★ ★
Hotel Type: Business resort
The Brief: Complete refurbishment /
Create a design concept for a room
Floor area incl. bathrooms: 34.64 m²

The preservation and refurbishment of this historical hunting lodge close to Berlin has resulted in a unique interior design with a style rarely encountered in Germany: in keeping with the hotel's rural setting and its heritage value, the rooms have been fitted exclusively with Shaker furnishings and design elements.

Created by the followers of a now practically defunct American religious community that shared all its worldly possessions, the distinctive craftsmanship of the Shaker style has left its mark in the annals of art history. With its stark lines, lack of ornamentation and functional design, Shaker furnishings anticipated core aspects of Modernist design long before its advent. A typical feature of Shaker furnishings is the peg rack, a practical solution for storing common objects.

This design offers guests a window to the spiritual world of the Shakers and combines wooden furnishings and fittings with clear lines. The room offers a new aesthetic experience that will reconnect guests with their inner balance.

A room in Shaker style – a hotel for reflection.

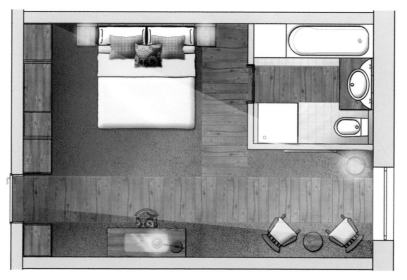

LakeSite Hotel
Fleesensee / Germany

Room Concept
Hotel Category: ★ ★ ★ ★
Hotel Type: : Resort hotel
The Brief: New building / Create a
design concept for a room
Floor area incl. bathrooms: 29.08 m²

This is a genuine lakeside hotel with panoramic views of the natural surroundings. Positioned in the centre of the room, the bed provides an unimpeded view of the lake. For once the television is a marginal detail – this design is all about the view.

The symmetrical design of the room features a bathroom divided into two areas with a separate toilet. On entering the room, guests are greeted by a real eye-catcher: a translucent glass wall which serves as a partitioning element. The motif on the screen reflects the hotel's idyllic rural setting: held between two plates of glass, grass and reeds swaying gently in the wind. This

semi-transparent signature piece offers guests their first glimpse of the stunning scenery. The room divider marks a transition and forms a discrete screen between the public and private areas.

Regionally sourced materials are used throughout the interior, cementing the bond between design and location. Cutting-edge technologies add a modern touch – fabrics replete with laser cutting and devoré effects offer a refreshing take on floral designs.

In the midst of nature – a room with a commanding lakeside view.

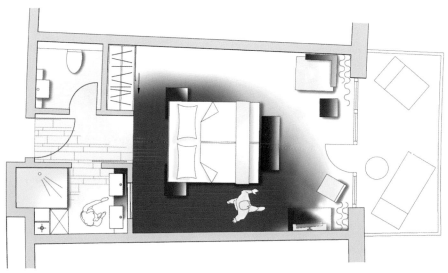

Landgasthof
Hanover / Germany

Room concept
Hotel Category: ★ ★ ★ ★
Hotel Type: Conference Hotel
The Brief: Complete renovation /
Designing a concept for a guest room
Floor area incl. bathrooms: 37.79 m²

There were plans to actually dismantle the country guesthouse, built in 1556, and transport it beam by beam to the United States, where it would be rebuilt. The plans changed, however, and the guesthouse was granted a new home near Hanover. After the common areas had been renovated, it was time to redesign the bedrooms.

The new design aimed to create spatial depth in the rooms and retain a mixture of old and new. The result is a tripartite design, each area characterized by differing flooring materials. On entering we first encounter a public space, followed by the 'quiet zone' surrounding the bed, and fi-nally the living area and desk in front of the window, further distinguished by the exposed roof beams that frame the window. The historic substance is contrasted with a modern glass bath enclosure. The toilet, designed as a separate room within the transparent bathroom area, is the only closed-off space in the room. At the centre of the room, conceptually and spatially, is the bed, which creates a calming transition between the common space and the living space at the window.

A single room in three parts: spatial zones as a bridge between zeitgeist and tradition.

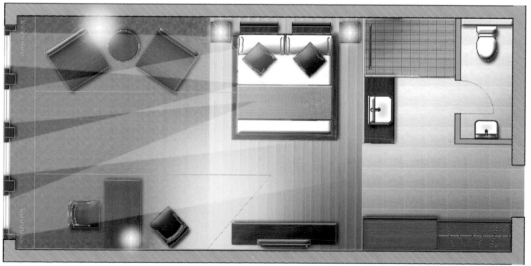

Le Méridien Grand Hotel
Nuremberg / Germany

Junior Suite Concept
Hotel Category: ★ ★ ★ ★ ★
Hotel Type: City hotel
(built at the turn of the last century)
The Brief: Complete refurbishment
of all existing rooms/suites /
Design concept for a Junior Suite
Floor area incl. bathrooms: 43.57 m²

Thoroughly European, this hotel draws on contemporary arts and culture to communicate modern identity without breaking with tradition. The sophisticated refinement of this design is readily apparent in the details, which evoke the spirit of countless European luxury brands. European guests will inevitably think of Coco Chanel when they see the black/white chequer-patterned fabrics, while the leather details and metal corners of the side table, mini-bar and bedside table are reminiscent of the signature works of Louis Vuitton. The elaborate quilting adorning the headboard evokes yet another European classic, the Barbour jacket. The congenial combination of this eye-catching feature and the racing green of the writing desk adds a splash of English style.

The room is just what one would expect from a traditional Grand Hotel, while also meeting the demands of the modern zeitgeist. The iPod docking stations on the bedside tables allow guests to personalise their hotel experience with their own music, and ensure they are awoken at the right time the next morning.

A room concept that communicates traditional European values in the here and now.

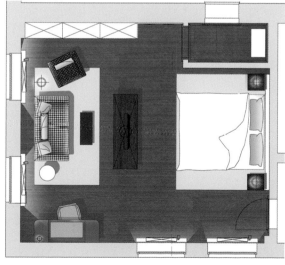

Room Design 'Next Step'
Hotel Category: ★ ★ ★ ★ ★
Hotel Type: City hotel
(built at the turn of the last century)
The Brief: Complete renovation of
all rooms and suites /
Create a design concept for a room
Floor area incl. bathrooms: 16.45 m²

Travellers are on a voyage of discovery: every day a different city, a different language and different culture. No place resembles another. The overriding theme at all places along the traveller's route is cartography – it leads, diverts, reveals trails and creates a connection with the local area, simultaneously representing motion and location.

The next step adds a new design feature: floor coverings mirror the theme of travel just as the old map reflects tradition and history. Its expanded dimensionality encompasses and tightly unifies the design. Asymmetric pendant lighting underscores motion, lightness and ease. In contrast, the substantial table lamps anchor motion to achieve balance. Behind the bed is a similarly enlarged motif: an ancient compass in a silvered frame picks up the travel theme and grounds the design. A variety of room layouts called for a differentiated approach to the room design. For example, in this relatively small room the cabinet doors are mirrored to visually enlarge the room and open up new perspectives.

Grounding: visual synonyms for travel.

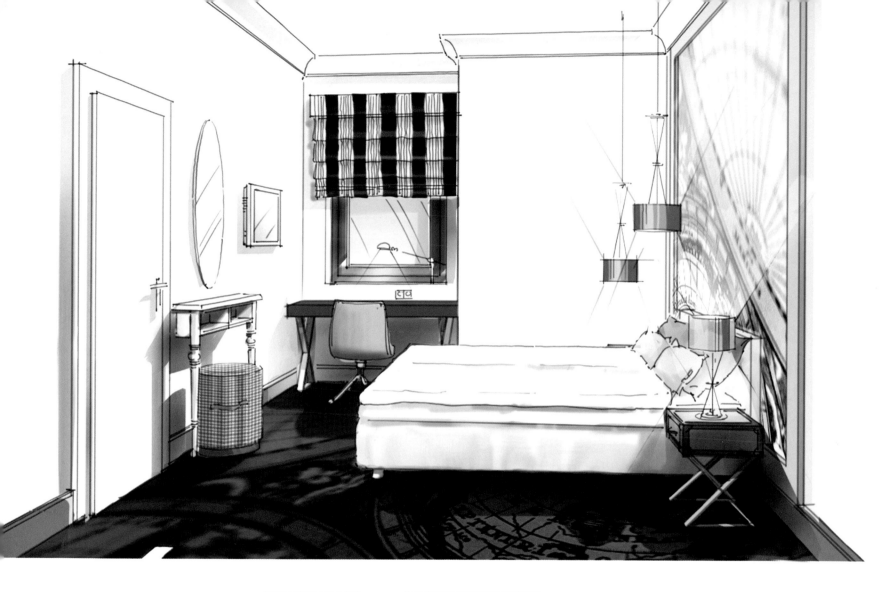

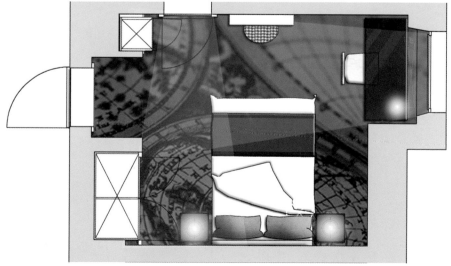

Le Méridien Parkhotel
Frankfurt Main / Germany

Room Concept 'fresh'
Hotel Category: ★ ★ ★ ★
Hotel Type: City hotel
The Brief: Complete refurbishment / Design concept for a Guest Room
Floor area incl. bathrooms: 22.10 m²

Le Méridien currently possesses one of the clearest and most successful brand statements in the global hotel industry, but was still evolving when the refurbishment of the rooms at the new section of the Parkhotel commenced. Previous design experiments included an opulently elegant French design, and an austere, cool solution from Art + Tech. At the time, the brand had recently been acquired by Starwood, which planned to make Le Méridien a bastion of European style within its group of companies. Irrespective of this brand philosophy, the small rooms called for a design with clear lines, a reserved style, light colours, little ornamentation and few patterns.

Two design options for this room were developed and constructed:
The design concept FRESH
and the colour scheme SOFT.
Both designs feature accent stripes on the walls and light maple fittings. The latter accommodates a television and serves as a mount for a glass etching above the bed.

Young and elegant design: A fitting addition to the vibrant city of Frankfurt.

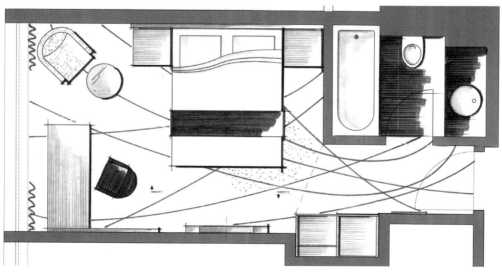

Room Concept 'soft'
Hotel Category: ★ ★ ★ ★ ★
Hotel Type: City hotel
The Brief: Complete refurbishment /
Design concept for a Guest Room
Floor area incl. bathrooms: 22.10 m^2

'fresh' concept:

Blue accent stripes, translucent blue drapes, light maple fittings, cream white walls and carpeting combine to produce a room design that is uniquely refreshing. Everything is light, smooth, round and flowing. A glass etching floats on a horizontal blue accent line, illuminated by the blue light mounted on the headboard below. The television can be conveniently hidden from view behind a stylish blue wall panel. The furnishings are distinctively light and appear to float gently above the floor. The carpeting features a soft colour scheme with an expressive pattern that adds a dynamic atmosphere to the room.

'soft' concept:

The furnishings used here are essentially identical to those used in the 'fresh' design. In the 'soft' concept the monochrome accent stripes seen in the other design have been replaced by discretely patterned surfaces featuring a tone-in-tone colour scheme for a more subtle and elegant effect. The colour scheme of the carpeting is similar to that used in the "Fresh" concept, but instead of the striking linear motif this design features an abstract floral theme. The result is a significantly cosier design featuring the same furnishings and with minimal changes to the colour scheme and textures.

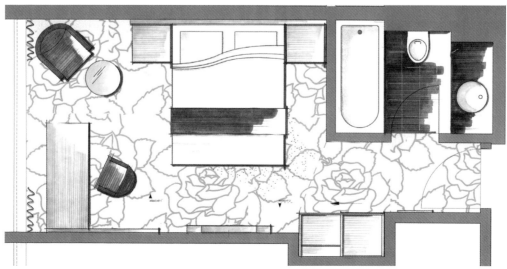

Les Jardins d'Alysea
Roeser / Luxembourg

Comfort Suite in Country Manor Style
Hotel Category: ★ ★ ★ ★ ★
Hotel Type: Senior residence
The Brief: New building / Create a design concept for a room
Floor area incl. bathrooms: 32.70 m²

Nestled in a beautiful valley in Roeser, in the south of Luxemburg, this retirement home is not only situated in a picturesque park landscape, but, through its plant-covered façade, merges with the natural landscape.

The brief here understandable involved extending the natural theme indoors. Not an easy task in a setting so authentically 'natural'. Of course, our understanding of nature is synonymous with the key requirement of hospitality design: to create spaces that are welcoming and evoke positive feelings. Parquet flooring in combination with carpeting in an abstract grey/beige leaf pattern forms the basis of an elegantly reserved design that picks up the colours and several themes of nature.

The golden yellow of sunshine and wheat fields, leaf green, oranges and reds of autumn sunsets as well as the theme of a soothing forest canopy seen from the treetops sets the tone in a photomontage installed above the bed.

As this design was created especially for older people, there is plenty of space in the room to avoid bumping a walking frame, along with a disability-friendly bathroom.

Nature brought into the room.

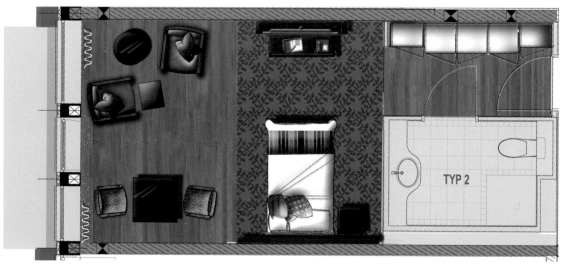

TYP 2

121

Les Jardins d'Alysea
Roeser / Luxembourg

Apartment Concept
Hotel Category: ★ ★ ★ ★ ★
Hotel Type: Senior residence
The Brief: New building
'La Residence & Les Villas' / Create a
design concept for an apartment
Floor area incl. bathrooms: 111.44 m²

A very clearly delineated, geometrical architecture and natural earth-tone colours distinguish this design. As soon as guests enter they encounter the room divider with its particularly interesting surface design. Behind this is a wardrobe. Also centrally located in the private lobby is a side table. Beyond this the room opens up into the interconnecting dining, fireplace and living room areas. The natural stone fireplace lends spatial character and serves as a segmenting element between the dining and living areas. Next to this is the exit to the large, private patio.

The spacious open floor plan is emphasised by the use of the same flooring materials throughout (oak parquet), though the patterns vary between the hall and lobby and the living and dining areas. A top-class suite such as this naturally includes two bedrooms, each with its own bathroom, not to mention a fully functional kitchen. The design plays with the juxtaposition of classical modernism and modern traditionalism, and, through the choice of colours, materials and textures, remains down-to-earth yet elegant.
A luxurious stay in a home of one's own.

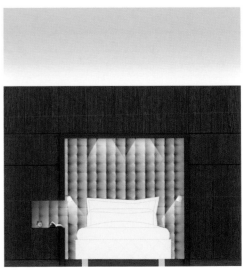

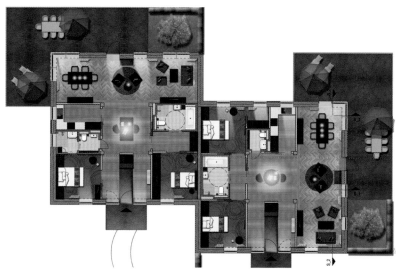

Linden Suites
Berlin / Germany

Suite Concept

Hotel Category: ★ ★ ★ ★ ★ superior
Hotel Type: City hotel
The Brief: Complete renovation / Design concept for two attached suites
Floor area incl. bathrooms: 112.70 m²

A kinship with Austria gives this hotel its special flair. With their focus on Viennese classicism, located far from big-city bustle, the Linden Suites transport guests into an oasis of calm. Soft grey/beige tones are paired with lively black and white, featuring individual lime-green accents. Austere stripes breathe new life into classic gentility. Crystal chandeliers and antique mirrors with polished glass frames reinvigorate classic themes, and Viennese wickerwork panels bridge the gap between the Spree and the Danube. Guests to this room are invited to tune out and turn inward.

The two suites have a shared entrance area. The larger of the two boasts an integrated fireplace in the centre of the room and a more spacious living and dining area. If the suites are occupied by two separate parties, the entrances will be divided by a partition, and the double-winged entrance area in the middle remains shut. If the two suites are booked together, all connecting doors are left open.

The charm of Vienna in Berlin – a night spent in elegance.

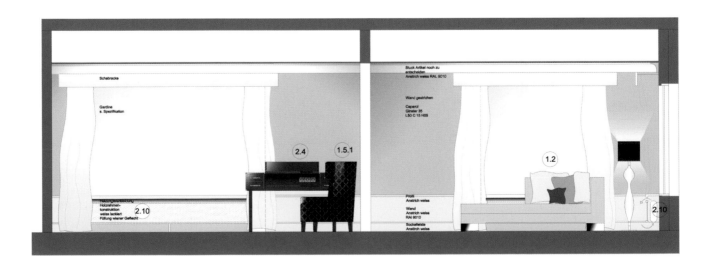

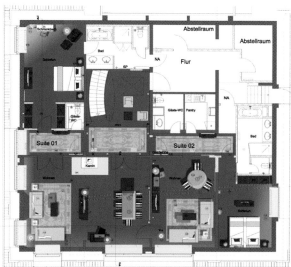

Lindner Park-Hotel Hagenbeck
Hamburg / Germany

Room Concept 'Africa'
Hotel Category: ★ ★ ★ ★ superior
Hotel Type: Urban hotel
The Brief: New building /
Design for the room type 'Africa'
Floor area incl. bathrooms: 26.18 m²

This hotel is located right next to one of Germany's most famous and innovative zoos. Guests can hear, smell, and sometimes even see the animals! The aim of the room design was to bring the animals' countries of origin alive and to put guests in the ideal frame of mind for a day at this zoo. The idea is to give guests a taste of the exotic, appealing to all of their sense. This should be a hotel stay to remember! The public areas on the ground-floor are designed in a colonial style, reflecting how the history of this zoo began. The zoo was founded in the nineteenth century, the first animals arriving by ship at Hamburg port.

The African rooms come alive with the atmosphere of life in the bush. Rustic natural elegance meets modern technology, with TV and telephone discreetly integrated into the exotic design. Much attention has been paid to detail: for example, an old suitcase in the entrance area doubles as a luggage rack, and the washbasins imitate the patterns of the African bongo antelope!

This side of Africa – a room full of animal magic.

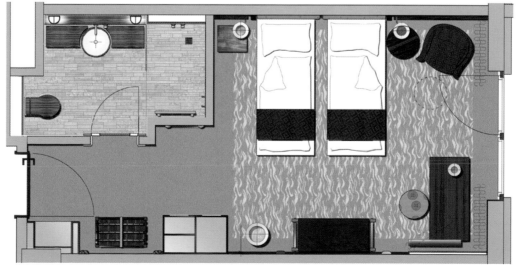

Lindner Park-Hotel Hagenbeck
Hamburg / Germany

Room Concept 'Asia'
Hotel Category: ★ ★ ★ ★ superior
Hotel Type: Urban hotel
The Brief: New building / Create a design concept for the room type 'Asia'
Floor area incl. bathrooms: 26.13 m²

What's the best way to get from Africa to Asia? By sea, of course! The 'Asia' rooms are situated on the upper floors of the hotel, accessible via an elevator that resembles a ship's cabin; guests select continents rather than floor numbers, then watch as their 'voyage' is tracked in moving points of light. That's why, when they check in, guests are not told which floor they are staying on, but in which continent.

On the upper floors an Asian-themed corridor leads guests to their rooms. There they encounter a world fashioned of bamboo and hand-carved wood, with marvellous balloon-shaped lighting fixtures. Fabrics are richly decorated and embroidered to recreate the colour and feel of Asia. As a counterpart to the rich variety of design themes in this hotel, one detail recurs in every room: the old suitcase reminiscent of journeys undertaken. The bathroom also contains an abundance of wood, and once again the washbasin is the centre of attention. In this case guests get to wash their faces and hands in a hollowed-out Asian boulder.

A cure for wanderlust: Asian enchantment in Hamburg.

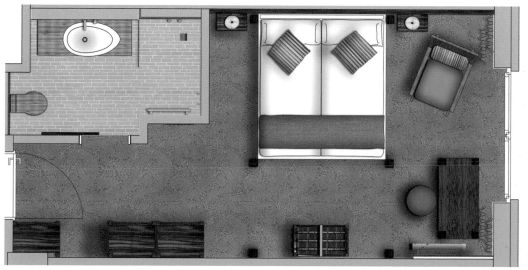

Lindner Park-Hotel Hagenbeck
Hamburg / Germany

Suite Concept 'Asia'
Hotel Category: ★ ★ ★ ★ superior
Hotel Type: Urban hotel
The Brief: New building / Design for the Asia Suites
Floor area incl. bathrooms: 95.73 m²

The hotel at Hagenbeck's Zoo in Hamburg is also geared towards conventioneers. There are many options here: the prominent conference centre with its pagoda-style roof offers a large ballroom and conference rooms that can be flexibly arranged. This is the perfect place either to throw a big party or to hold a conference. The colonial-themed ground floor meets the requirements of both. The rooms here are decorated in the styles of the world's continents. Most luxurious of all are the suites intended for longer stays.

The Asia Suites lead guests into an enchanted world of pattern, ornamentation and wood carvings. What began as a mere hotel stay becomes a journey of discovery. The common area invites guests to relax in a rocker and provides space for videoconferencing. It transitions then into a spacious bathroom, where a smooth pebble floor provides a sensuous foot massage. The highpoint of this room design is its depth. Guests reach their own private spa area via the walk-through dressing area. This is a great place to step out of everyday life and hatch a few new plans.

Pure Asia – dive into another world.

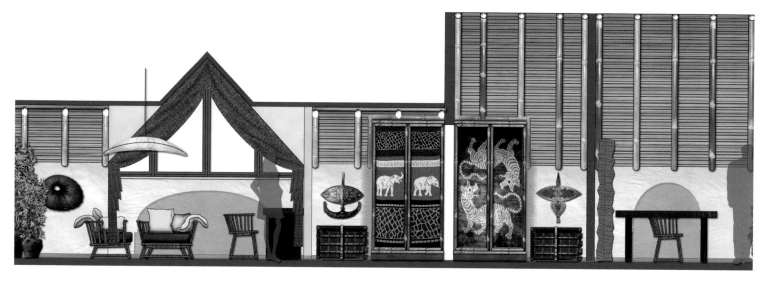

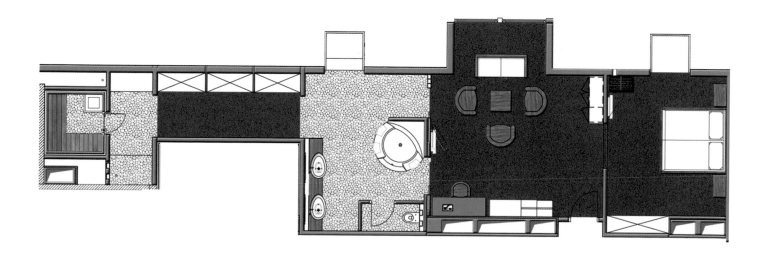

Luxury Hotel
Bonn / Germany

Room Concept
Hotel Category: ★ ★ ★ ★ ★ superior
Hotel Type: Conference hotel
The Brief: New building /
Create a design concept for a room
Floor area incl. bathrooms: 30.72 m²

The architecture of this new hotel on the banks of the Rhine maximises the spectacular views of the river: full-length glazing in the rooms connects guests with their natural surroundings. The calm, easy flow of this magnificent river provides the perfect backdrop for mobile working and high-powered conferences. The interior colour scheme is designed to complement the hotel's natural surroundings and features a stylish shade of cream combined with soft natural hues and wooden surfaces. The design features a range of subtle structures and textures that will enchant guests. The layout is striking and unconventional: positioned in the centre of the room, the bed faces the window and backs onto the bathroom, which forms a transparent cube within the room. Guests are presented with a clear view of the river the moment they enter the room. With a separate room for the toilet, the design is open and flexible – individual elements are scattered about like stones on a riverbed. Modern and multicultural: a bookcase houses a collection of holy texts from around the globe, giving equal weight to each religious tradition.

A forward-looking design concept – open and unconventional.

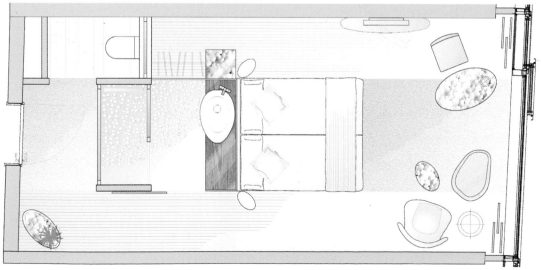

Room Concept 'Next Step'

Hotel Category: ★ ★ ★ ★ – ★ ★ ★ ★ ★

Hotel Type: Conference hotel

The Brief: New building /
Create a design concept for a room

Floor area incl. bathrooms: 24.19 m²

This variation plays with the cubic form of the bathroom to achieve a more conventional layout. The furniture encircles the centre of the room, which is occupied by the bed, imbuing this area with the same spacious character.

This room has a more colourful and distinctive style. A range of natural colours and refined brown tones sets off the accent colour of the organic armchair – an eye-catcher par excellence. The intelligent design of the bathroom's exterior surfaces lends it the same open quality: the entrance is positioned between two transparent wardrobe elements and a

glass front opens onto the room, softening the impression of the cube and making it seem almost weightless. Mounted on a wooden surface, the shape of the wash basin resembles a softly rounded pebble on a riverbed and reflects the natural style of this design. Parquet flooring and woollen rugs underscore the unabashedly organic flavour of the room and contrast with the dynamic forms of the contemporary furniture elements.

A down-to-earth variation with an open style that plays with conventions.

Maris Resort
Turkey

Room Concept
Hotel Category: ★ ★ ★ ★ ★ superior
Hotel Type: Holiday hotel complex
The Brief: New building /
Designing a concept for a guest room
Floor area incl. bathrooms: 27.12 m²

Set atop a stunning bay on the Turkish Aegean, this hotel complex imparts to its guests a sense of the country and its people, with Ottoman patterns and echoes of Turkish culture as decoration. Guests have the opportunity to delve into Turkey, exploring a different culture and customs as a welcome break from everyday life. In addition to the comforts offered by all hotels in this chain, here guests are transported into a world of extravagant elegance.
The room features a patchwork of tile and parquet flooring, trimmed in contrasting colours. A slender aisle leads the guest into the room, culminating in an oasis of calm facing the windows. This oriental lounge is the perfect place to read a book or watch the sunset with a loved one. The rounded forms of the furniture are reflected and continued in the ornamentally etched glass window that separates the bathroom and bedroom, letting natural light into the bath area and acting as an eye-catching feature in the room.

A room rooted in Ottoman patterns and colours – reflecting a different land and different customs.

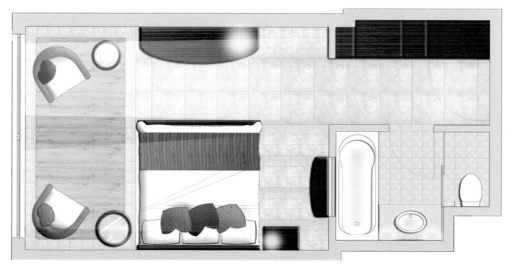

Mercure Hotel & Residenz
Frankfurt Main / Germany

Room Concept 'MainLINE'
Hotel Category: ★ ★ ★ ★
Hotel Type: City hotel / business hotel
The Brief: Complete refurbishment of all rooms and suites / Design concept for a room
Floor area incl. bathrooms: 30.71 m²

In the German imagination the city of Frankfurt conjures up visions of high-rise buildings and skyscrapers. Architecture is structure and texture; the materials are stone, concrete, glass, and steel. The room design is distinguished by its sensitive take on this local theme: "metropolitan cool" contrasts with an orange accent, giving the room an aura of warmth and cosiness while discretely alluding to the colourful neon signage and disco lights of the big city. Coloured light underscores this effect and accentuates the leitmotif of this design – a curved wall separating the bathroom and living area. Breaking with the geometric tone of the room, the wall lends the interior a lively and dynamic note. This is design that lives and breathes – just like the city of Frankfurt. The bathroom is another key element. More than just a sanitary facility, this is a "room with a view", where guests can greet the new day through a panorama window that will appeal to their sense of freedom.

A hotel room that captures the spirit of Frankfurt – a cosmopolitan, dynamic, and yet very intimate place.

138

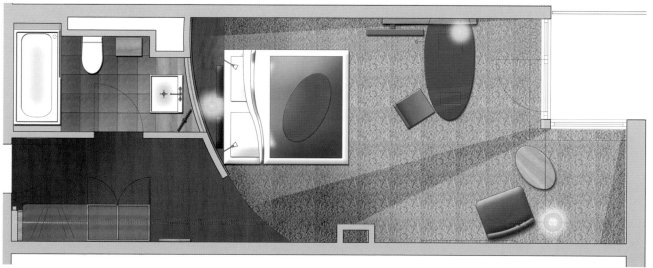

Mercure Hotel
Krefeld / Germany

Room Concept

Hotel Category: ★ ★ ★ ★ superior

Hotel Type: Conference hotel

The Brief: Complete refurbishment of all rooms and suites / Design concept for a room

Floor area incl. bathrooms: 25.96 m²

Adjoining a golf course, this conference hotel in Krefeld throws open its doors to golfers on the weekends, and hosts conference guests throughout the week. The hotel offers both groups of guests a sensuous and stylish experience. The design speaks to the senses in a complex dialogue in which quality is king. The Mercure Hotel in Krefeld steals the show with top-class hospitality packaged in a sensuous and clear design.

Blending a playful floral motif with a strict geometric layout, the rooms communicate an elegance that will be appreciated by business guests and golfers alike. The abstract floral motif printed on the carpeting resembles a "runner" and, combined with the green accents and elegant design, infuses the room with a soothing, natural aura that will help guests switch off and recover from a day of sensory overload. The reassuring clear lines of the design will make guests feel instantly at home.

A room designed to soothe.

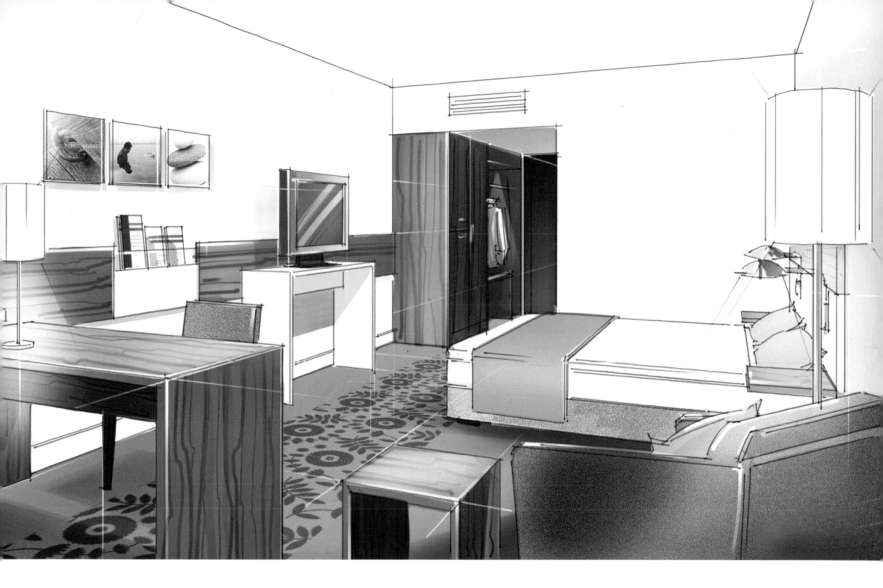

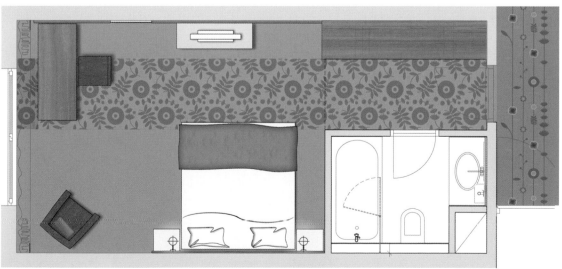

Mercure Hotel Stuttgart
Stuttgart Bad Cannstatt / Germany

Room Concept
Hotel Category: ★ ★ ★ superior
Hotel Type: Business hotel
The Brief: Guest room refurbishment /
Design concept for a room
Floor area incl. bathrooms: 21.22 m²

What do conference guests desire most after enduring the hardship of a marathon session dominated by computers and artificial lighting? Flowing water, green meadows, and relaxation!

This design for the Mercure Hotel in Bad Cannstatt has a natural flair: the headboard features a grassy motif and the blue desk captures the beauty of the nearby Neckar River. This is a haven to unwind in after a day among the bustle of a public event.

The original floor plan included the bay window and relatively tight layout. The bed and armchair are positioned on the same side of the room, allowing guests to watch television from either and resulting in an unusual layout – the bed is positioned at an angle in front of the window and the armchair against the wall to the bathroom.

The design opens up the room, creating a more spacious feeling than the previous design.

Set at an angle to the wall, the headboard dominates the visual design; the furnishings and fixtures are accordingly low key, but oh-so-stylish.

A room of many angles: An invitation to relax.

Mid-scale Guest Room Concept
Marseille / France

Room Concept 'Art'
Hotel Category: ★ ★ ★ – ★ ★ ★ ★
Hotel Type: Conference hotel
The Brief: Complete refurbishment / Create a design concept for a room
Floor area incl. bathrooms: 20.47 m²

Numerous hotels from a single chain required complete refurbishment. The challenge was to create an inspiring new look with a warm atmosphere on a small budget. The solution: details were created using graphic elements, while the playful contours of the furnishings create delightful optical illusions. The seemingly real "table legs", for instance, are silhouettes that have been carefully milled into the surface. The result is a charming blend of illusion and reality.

This design takes a playful approach to French culture and the fine arts that is best embodied by the gigantic picture frame above the bed. The multifunctional furnishings provide a perfect solution to the compact floor plan: the footrest for the armchair doubles as a comfortable desk chair, for instance. The design of the desk has been pared down to its barest minimum – modern business nomads travel light and prefer to use their notebooks in the comfort of an armchair. The side table stands alone and provides an additional surface beside the desk for depositing keys and other personal belongings.

Trompe L'Oeil: a room that transforms visions into reality.

Room Concept "Provence"
Hotel Category: ★ ★ ★ – ★ ★ ★ ★
Hotel Type: Conference hotel
The Brief: Complete refurbishment /
Create a design concept for a room
Floor area incl. bathrooms: 20.47 m²

This design was inspired by the capital of Provence, Marseille. The room has a traditionally Provençal flavour that evokes the dazzling beauty and sweet scent of its lavender fields. This is a design that invites guests to immerse themselves in another world. Featuring typically French architectural elements, the fixtures include a wrought iron balcony railing, basketwork, embroidery, plaid fabrics and lace. The variations also feature the same stylistic elements as the other design concepts of this series: the balcony railing on the wall above the bed is a painted silhouette and the bedside table legs are 2-D cutaways.

The design offers a succinct translation of traditional styles within a contemporary setting.
A stunning image in the bathroom steals the show: this large format print of lavender fields extends across two surfaces. The print provides the perfect backdrop for guests to unwind in the evening and will add an invigorating splash of colour to their morning. Small is beautiful: a new age dawns in the revamped bathroom.

The colour purple – a truly Provençal room.

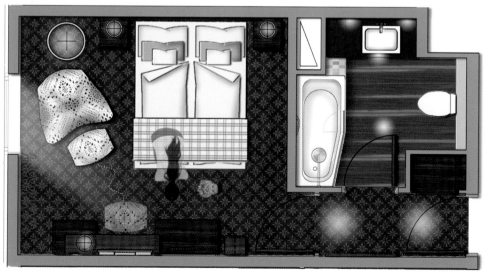

Room Concept "Yacht"
Hotel Category: ★ ★ ★ − ★ ★ ★ ★
Hotel Type: Conference hotel
The Brief: Complete refurbishment /
Create a design concept for a room
Floor area incl. bathrooms: 20.47 m²

As the hotel is located directly adjacent to the marina, a maritime theme was a must for the third design concept. Marseille's gift to the world: enjoy your bouillabaisse with a view of the marina! With this room guests can embark on a grand tour of the oceans. The leather upholstery of the deck chair has all the flair of a luxury yacht. The carpet is one step ahead: a stylised jetty guides guests through the room and out onto the deck. The ship's railing above the bed promises sweet dreams – like a maritime lullaby, it evokes a deep a sense of security. But all is not what it seems: this panoramic view is merely a painting and the table legs are in fact cut out of the surface.

Refreshing and pure: the image in the bathroom invites guests to take the plunge and indulge their senses! A refreshing bath will help guests forget their cares and wash away their worries. This is a place to recharge your batteries and look forward to whatever tomorrow might bring!

Welcome aboard – a maritime hotel room.

148

'Modu X'
Guest Room Concept

Room Concept
Hotel Category: ★ ★ ★ ★
Hotel Type: Business hotel
The Brief: New building /
Create a design concept for a room
Floor area incl. bathrooms: 28,10 m²

From city hotels and holiday resorts, to business and leisure hotels – this modular system is highly versatile and can be easily adapted to any setting! The quadratic form of its rounded wooden frame can be decorated with a range of materials, including wickerwork, glass, wood, metal, leather and fabrics. Flexibility is the watchword: optional headboard designs include an upholstered surface set in a wooden frame, a back-lit surface with wickerwork, and stainless steel panels adorned with quality fabrics. The wardrobe doors and desk accessories follow a similar design.

Each room has its own special character and can be easily adapted as required! Guests travel more widely with every passing year and their expectations are constantly changing in light of these experiences – the flexibility afforded by this system will enable hotel operators to "dress up" their rooms by changing the colour scheme and materials as required: a complete facelift in the wink of an eye.

A modular design – a room like a chameleon.

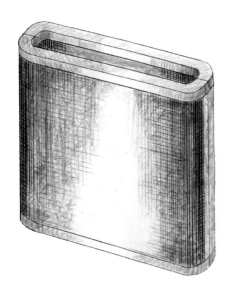
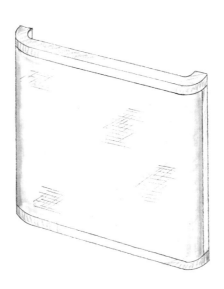
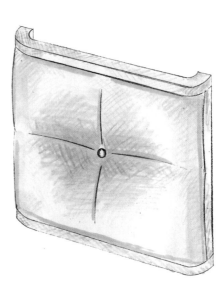

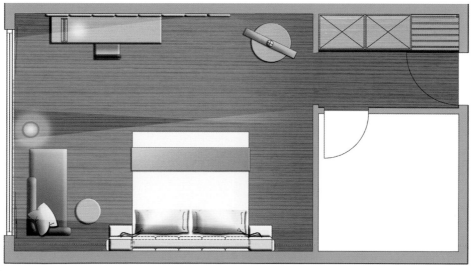

Mövenpick Hotel
Munich-Airport / Germany

Room Concept 'Outside IN'
Hotel Category: ★ ★ ★ ★
Hotel Type: Airport hotel
The Brief: Total refurbishment of rooms and suites on the business floor / Create a design concept for a room
Floor area incl. bathrooms: 28.06 m²

The essence of this design concept is the idea of the hotel room as a place of refuge for a conference guest or airline passenger. Through its cubic, linear forms and the interplay of different tones of grey, brown and beige, the room conveys a calm and peaceful atmosphere.

However, only on entering the bathroom does the uniqueness of this design concept become apparent. This, after all, is the space in which guests prepare, mentally and physically, for the day ahead, and where they relax and recuperate in the evenings. This bathroom is a kind of indoor oasis, a place where guests escape from the cold steel and hot jet fumes of the airport, where they can relax and recharge their batteries. This room has a soothing effect: pine-green walls, sand-coloured tiles and warm walnut tones are the perfect antidote to the speed and stress of air travel.

The bedroom area contains splashes of colour that anticipate the explosion that takes place in the bathroom. 'Outside IN' thus reveals its true colours on the interior and undersides of various items of furniture.

Outside turned in – a hotel room that requires a second glance.

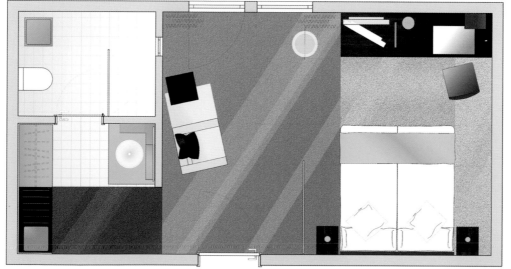

Mövenpick Hotel
Regensdorf / Switzerland

Room Design 'be nature'
Hotel Category: ★ ★ ★ ★
Hotel Type: Conference hotel
The Brief: Complete renovation / Create a design concept for a room
Floor area incl. bathrooms: 27.20 m²

At this conference hotel located conveniently close to Zurich airport guests look for a peaceful, relaxing room to help them decompress after jet fumes and the convention. Nature is the perfect counterpoint. The new room arrangements reinforce the tranquility factor.

A totally new hotel room experience emerges here through use of unconventional living and sleeping zones. Just as a reading chair is normally positioned next to a window, the sleeping area with bed and nightstands typically adjoin the bathroom. Here the arrangement was entirely reconceived with the sleeping area placed in the quietest zone of the room. An unusually spacious area emerges adjacent to the bathroom where the living area divides the room into public and private zones. The impression of spaciousness is emphasized by the full-length mirror that leans against the wall. At the interface between the public and private areas, the floor and wall coverings change. The transition is palpable – two room zones merging to form a larger whole.

A harmonious blend of nature and technology.

Room Design 'be culture'
Hotel Category: ★ ★ ★ ★
Hotel Type: Conference hotel
The Brief: Complete renovation /
Create a design concept for a room
Floor area incl. bathrooms: 21.81 m²

This is a design concept intended for hotels located in the countryside rather than at transportation nodes, airports or in a metropolis. Guests who attend a conference in a greenbelt justifiably expect peaceful, natural surroundings. They would like the room to provide inspiration, stimulation and to serve as a source of ideas. The floors and walls encourage these ideas through the use of printed texts.

'be culture' introduces a cultural aspect through this particular design by juxtaposing the texts of local authors, thus adding a touch of local colour. The surfaces of the room offer the guest an additional benefit: a bedtime story! Contemporary technology makes it all possible as floor and wall covering manufacturers now offer individualized prints.

What's more, the layout of the room is reversed, with the bed against the window and the area in front of it as an open, more public zone. Guests can thus invite business colleagues and new contacts up to their room without worrying that the visitors will feel uncomfortable about invading their privacy.

Cultured surfaces – a room with its own bedtime story.

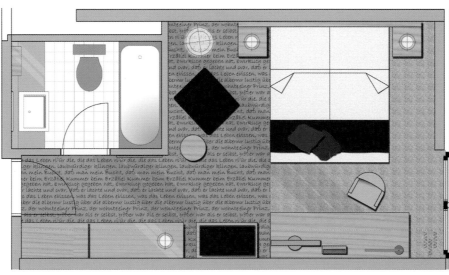

NH Hotel
Frankfurt Niederrad, Germany

Room Concept

Hotel Category: ★ ★ ★ ★ superior
Hotel Type: Business hotel
The Brief: New building / Create a design concept for a room
Floor area incl. bathrooms: 18.72 m²

This was the first new hotel building in Germany to be designated as an 'NH Hotel'. However, as the rooms were originally planned for a Tulip Inn, they were simply too small. In particular, because of the floor plan the entrance areas provided no room for a closet.

The diagonal layout of the bed and furnishings create new angles and corners, adding functionality to the room. The defining angle is formed by the bed. On the desk opposite is the television, which by its location forms part of the "work corner". The "corner" next to the bed is intended for relaxation, with a lamp and side table as well as a recliner in full view of the TV. The third corner has been made into a closet area. Because the line of the bathroom is extended to provide an additional corner for drawers, something of an open walk-in closet is created – in a room that originally had no space for one. A recessed niche behind the bed acts as a night table.

A distinguished business hotel room accommodated within a limited space.

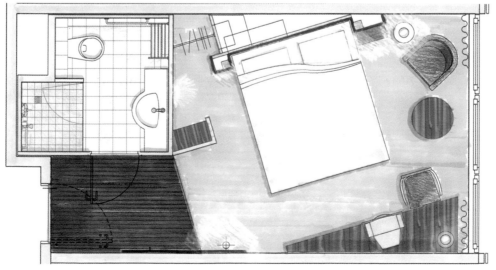

Nordsee Resorthotel
Keitum on the Island of Sylt / Germany

Junior Suite Concept
Hotel Category: ★ ★ ★ ★ ★ superior
Hotel Type: Resort hotel
The Brief: New building /
Design concept for a junior suite
Floor area incl. bathrooms: 43.08 m²

This new hotel on the North Sea island of Sylt was built from scratch, but follows a traditional design with a thatched roof and white plastered walls. Naturally, the interior also called for a design solution that introduces modern accents while remaining true to the roots of this place. After all, guests holidaying on the island don't want to take leave of the modern conveniences and comforts they enjoy at home.

The resulting design is a classic: a hotel room that is contemporary yet reminiscent of the island's history. The bathroom has been designed in a relatively open way, offering guests the maximum in comfort augmented by a cleverly positioned opening that allows a commanding view of the room from the antique-styled bathtub. The adjoining toilet also opens to the communal area, thus serving as a guest bathroom. The use of form is classic, the colour scheme is natural with maritime touches. A particular accent is set by the wooden jetty flooring between the living and sleeping areas.

Get that Sylt feeling: new spatial experiences in a historical context.

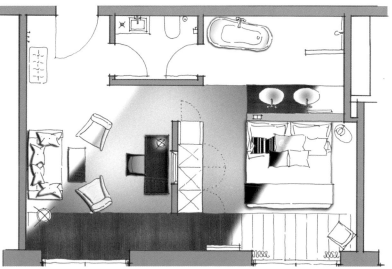

'Organic Trace'
Guest Room Concept

Room Concept
Hotel Category: ★ ★ ★ ★
Hotel Type: Business Hotel
The Brief: New building /
Designing a concept for a guest room
Floor area incl. bathrooms: 39.00 m²

This is a hotel room for the future. As the line between business and pleasure continues to blur, so do the traditional lines of a hotel room, as reflected in the sculptural design of this room. The bathtub moves to the centre of the room, a symbol of relaxation. Mimicking the movement of a wave, the bath swings in a wide arc to the bed, marking the desk in between. The sculpture sits in the room like a pebble on a riverbed, washed by the waves, ready for the demands of a new generation. The toilet is the only closed off room here, beyond the arching paraffin-hued wall.

Every element of this design is of one piece: desk, bed and walls are formed out of acrylic mineral material, formed to shape under heat. The surface is pleasantly soft and warm, and also durable and washable. Soft accents taken from nature complete the theme, such as the bonsai plant, wooden chair legs or textured fabrics.

Organic Trace: the hotel room as a sculpture.

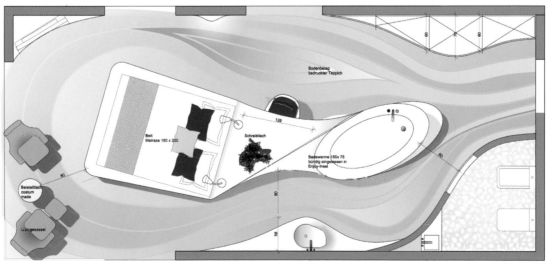

Ostseeresort
Ahlbeck in the Island of Usedom / Germany

Room Concept
Hotel Category: ★ ★ ★ ★ ★
Hotel Type: Resort hotel
The Brief: New building /
Create a design concept for a room
Floor area incl. bathrooms: 28.50 m²

Usedom: water, wind, golden sandy beaches, wicker beach chairs, and classic spas. Lightness: leave your cares behind, relax, and just be. A day on the island: wander along the beach with the warm sun on your back and the water caressing your legs, washing the sand from your bare feet. Forget about your e-mails – just be. The inspiring architecture of the Imperial Baths says it all – this is a place with its own history and traditions.

This hotel is the perfect place to enjoy the morning sunshine and unwind in the evenings. Guests can put their feet up and relax, or even write a postcard: the desk is

just the right size. The curving line of the sofa adds a gentle dynamic to the room and toys with Usedom's picturesque form. The colours are perfectly matched to the island: light and refreshing with a maritime flair. With its commanding view through the bedroom and towards the Baltic, the bathtub is the ideal place to end the day. This is a room to relax in.

The lightness of being – a room for the island.

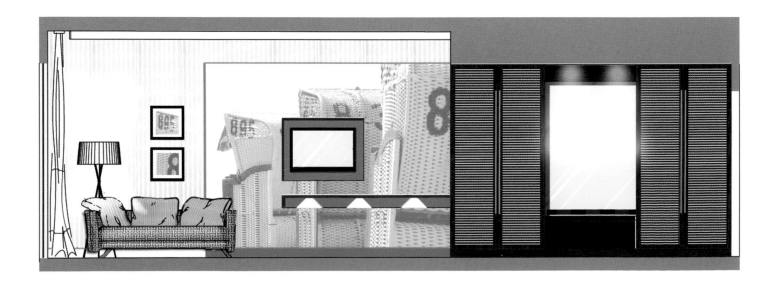

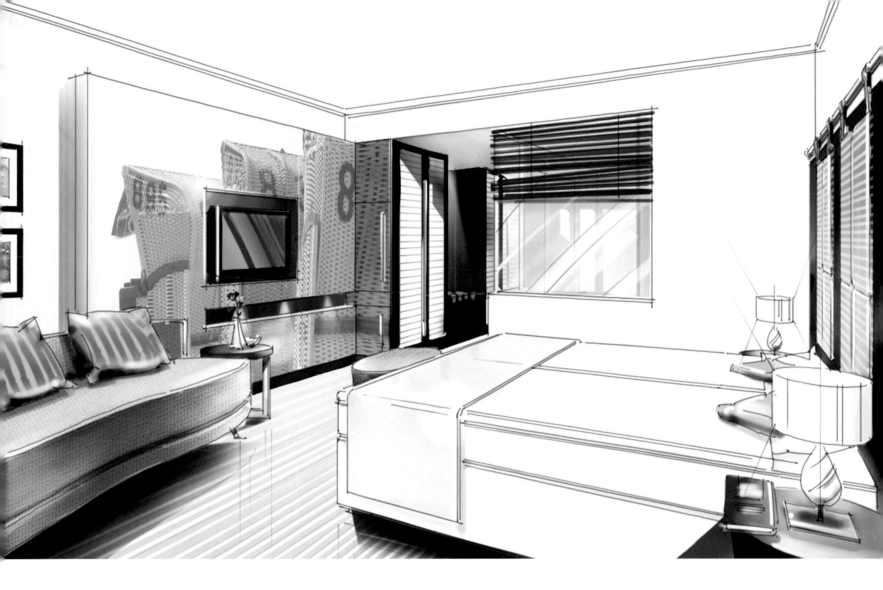

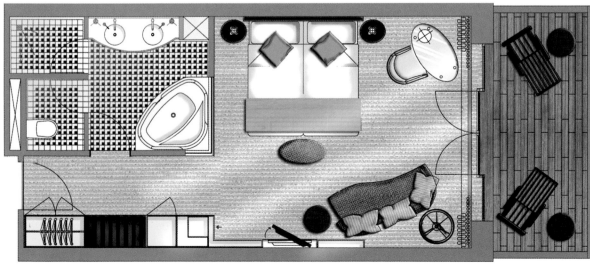

Hotel Palaisgarten
Baden-Baden / Germany

'Modern Sophisticated' Room Concept
Hotel Category: ★ ★ ★ ★ ★ superior
Hotel Type: City hotel
The Brief: Complete refurbishment /
Create a design concept for a room
Floor area incl. bathrooms: 31.00 m²

A hotel for Baden-Baden – a house with a history and the opulent style of times past. This hotel embodies a tradition of elegant repose and leisure that is synonymous with the name of Baden-Baden, Germany's foremost spa town. The refurbishment of the interior is set to revitalize the hotel, ensuring that younger and older guests will feel equally at home in an institution that has delighted generations of guests. Created as private retreats, the rooms in the original building ooze historical charm. This is 'Modern Sophisticated', a design that honours the past: the outer walls will not be altered, and all of the fittings and furnishings will be set back from the wall. Rather than seeking to create contrasts, the design successfully integrates historical elements within a contemporary hospitality experience. Drawing on poetry, dance, song and architecture, the tailor-made art concept showcases the best that present-day Baden-Baden has to offer, thereby building a bridge between the past and present.

Art connects – a Grand Hotel for our time.

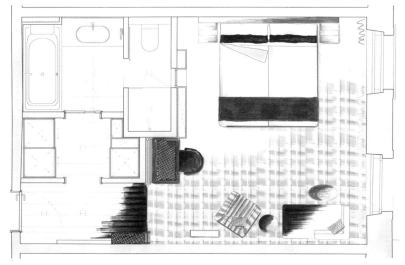

Hotel Palaisgarten
Baden-Baden / Germany

'Relaxed Classic' Room Concept
Hotel Category: ★ ★ ★ ★ ★ superior
Hotel Type: City hotel
The Brief: Extend the existing hotel /
Create a design concept for a room
Floor area incl. bathrooms: 31.00 m²

This hotel has a sombre charm and no doubt many guests will look forward to its refurbishment with a sense of foreboding rather than pleasant expectation. This hotel is an intimate retreat: guests revel in the unparalleled privacy afforded by the availability of thermal spring water in all of the rooms – a symbol of luxury and leisurely independence. The new look communicates the hotel's core values: luxury and intimacy.

The new extension lacks the historical charm of the main building and requires a more attentive approach – the solution: 'Relaxed Classic'. A tailor-made art concept infuses the rooms with all the pomp and elegance of times past, while the wood panelling lends the room an aristocratic touch. Old meets new: classic ornaments decorate the room, contrasting with the clear lines and depth of the contemporary surfaces. Drawing on a contemporary vocabulary, both concepts span the divide between very different epochs, ensuring that both new and regular guests will feel at home in this illustrious institution.

Relax and enjoy – a modern translation of times past.

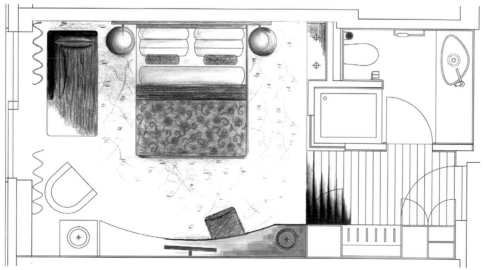

Palaishotel
Vienna / Austria

Suite Concept
Hotel Category: ★ ★ ★ ★ ★ superior
Hotel Type: City hotel
The Brief: Connecting wing and extension to the Palais / Design concept for a suite
Floor area incl. bathrooms: 63.02 m²

Capturing the magic of old Vienna was the aim for the new extension in the Stadtpalais gardens, an angular glass structure. Rooms were to be built here bridging the old and the new, transposing the old-world ambiance of the Palais onto the new building. A further challenge was a connecting wing between the buildings, a structure that once housed servants' quarters. How can continuity be created between these structures, maintaining the high expectations set by the main house?

The answer is as simple as it is clever: a modern interpretation of the design concept behind the main house. Curtains act as partitions, transporting individual stylistic elements into the present. The same stylistic approach is followed in all three buildings, with a different flourish in each case. Rooms are decorated in white and subtle gold tones, combined with gold-plated accents, golden mosaic tiles and translucent golden curtains. Guests wishing to glance out the window are in for a tactile treat: the frame is covered in button-tufted upholstery.

White and gold – a majestic bridge between past and present.

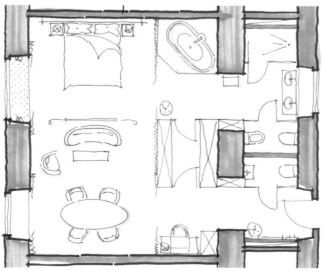

Park Hotel
Brussels / Belgium

Room Concept
Hotel Category: ★ ★ ★ ★
Hotel Type: Conference hotel
The Brief: Complete renovation /
Designing a concept for a guest room
Floor area incl. bathrooms: 25.86 m²

After a long day at a conference, guests staying at this forest hotel can look forward to relaxing in the extensive spa area. The room reflects the focus of the hotel, with a bathtub positioned in the room. Storage space abounds, with a comfy stool doubling as a suitcase stand. Opposite is the actual bath area, featuring a spacious shower and a window to the room. Etched floral patterns let daylight in, but only reveal silhouettes.

The design owes much to feng shui, with rounded corners and fine-grain bamboo flooring. The entrance area is floored in contrasting light stone. A full-length window opens to the park outside. Floral patterns are reflected in fabrics, bringing the outdoors inside. As doing without a television was not an option, even in a room so focused on wellness, a compromise was reached: A flatscreen on a swivel arm means the TV is mostly out of sight, but can still be positioned to take in the evening news while relaxing in the bathtub.

The green of nature inside – the hotel room as a refuge.

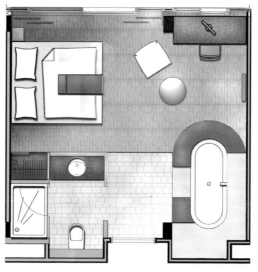

Park Hotel
Brussels / Belgium

Junior Suite Concept
Hotel Category: ★ ★ ★ ★
Hotel Type: Conference hotel
The Brief: Complete renovation /
Design concept for a junior suite
Floor area incl. bathrooms: 34.51 m²

This suite has an unusual layout, which was dictated by the existing structure. The sleeping and sitting areas are fully exposed to the park, which borders the hotel. The entrance area is accentuated by light stone flooring. A green band separates it from room, and continues upwards to form the desk, which frames the head of the bed in a protective gesture. Behind the desk is a walk-in closet. A transparent screen allows a view from the bathtub into the main room and beyond.

The room features an open floor plan and a focus on wellness and nature. Whether lying in bed or lounging on the sofa or armchairs, guests have the option of looking out at the park or watching television. The flatscreen TV is integrated into the wall, but can be hidden from sight using a fabric panel. With the sliding bathroom door open, the bathtub becomes a central part of the design and, owing to the glass screen, a focal point of the room.

The green band – the connection to nature.

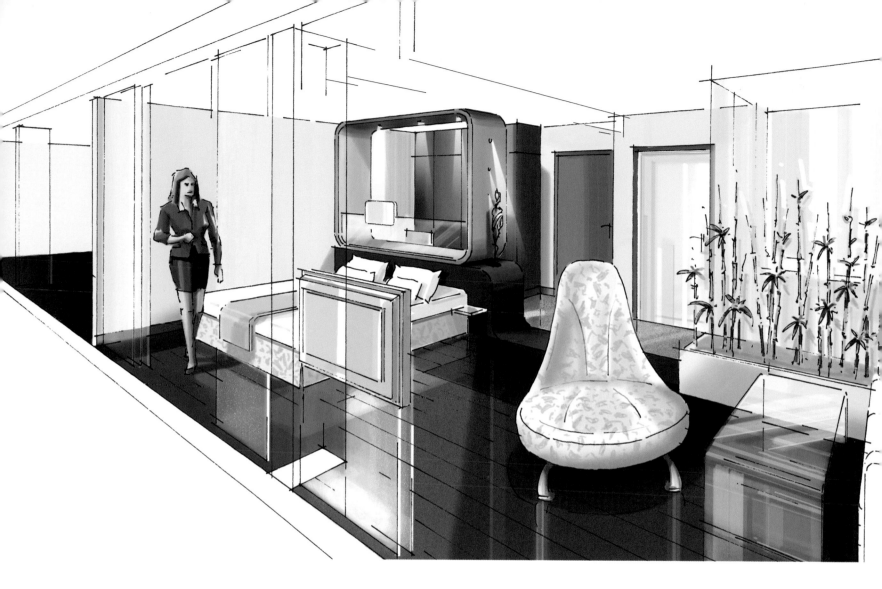

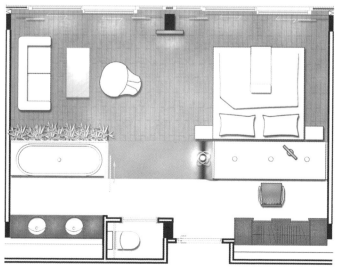

Park Inn Krakow
Krakow, Poland

Room Concept
Hotel Category: ★ ★ ★ ★
Hotel Type: Hotel in urban locale
The Brief: New construction / Guest room design
Floor area incl. bathrooms: 24.14 m²

The rooms at Krakow's Park Inn Hotel reflect the brand values of clarity, authenticity and honesty with their bright, genuine and open style. These qualities are found in Park Inn hotels throughout the world and provide guests with a feeling of familiarity. And yet the style is also customised to the character of the region, giving guests a sense of the locale. This young hotel brand is refreshing, open and full of energy. The Park Inn is a celebration of the primary colours: blue, red, yellow and green. The colour scheme is replicated throughout the hotel and reinforces the brand's character.

A sojourn at the Park Inn should be comfortable and uncomplicated – but above all enjoyable! The interior design is contemporary and will appeal to travellers, conventioneers, families and urban tourists alike. Guests may select a room themed in red for warmth and creativity or in blue for quiet relaxation. With its clear lines and elegant style the furniture ensemble remains modestly in the background, yet impresses through a number of intelligent details.

Brand design: a room shows its true colours.

'Purple Trace'
Guest Room Concept

Room Concept
Hotel Category: ★ ★ ★ ★ ★
Hotel Type: City hotel
The Brief: Complete refurbishment /
Create a design concept for a room
Floor area incl. bathrooms: 22.13 m²

A sign of the times: the interior draws on the rich history of this hotel, integrating vintage design elements in an enchanting blend of past and present. The solid wood fitted wardrobes have been retained and given a facelift by adding a new frontage. They testify to a long tradition of craftsmanship. The equally finely worked side table, with its detailed inlays, makes a natural counterpart – it has likewise been refurbished and restored to the room. The rich history of these elements connects the new interior with the previous design, creating a warm atmosphere that will delight regular guests returning to the revamped hotel.

This is a very contemporary historical hotel; historical elements are framed in a contemporary design with a distinctive colour scheme. The blackberry hue (hence 'Purple Trace') symbolizes the present and adds a decidedly modern elegance to the design. The white tone rounds off the colour scheme and completes this sophisticated blend of traditional and modernist design.

Connecting with the past: history in a contemporary design.

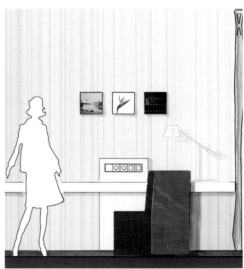

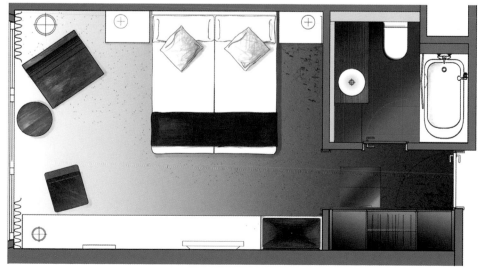

Pyramids Palace
Cairo / Egypt

Room Concept
Hotel Category: ★ ★ ★ ★ ★ superior
Hotel Type: Luxury hotel
The Brief: New building /
Create a design concept for a room
Floor area incl. bathrooms: 39.48 m²

A palace with a view of the pyramids of Giza: set in a breathtaking setting close to the Sphinx and the Nile, a hotel that invites you to explore Egyptian history and culture like never before. The hotel complex combines all the flair of its unique setting with the best that contemporary hotel design has to offer.

Taking its cue from the nearby pyramids, the focus of the room layout is at the centre of the room and will draw guests inwards. The diagonal line of the wall gently guides guests into the room and allows for a spacious bathroom entrance. The living and sleeping area is self-contained – a slid-ing door allows guests to adjust the view through to the foyer and bathroom as they please. The use of high-quality materials lends the design an unexpected subtlety as the materials set off the clear lines of the geometric floor plan to stunning effect. This is a carefully crafted design that is perfectly in keeping with the majestic style of this historically important site.

The power of the diagonal line – a palace in the shadow of the Sphinx.

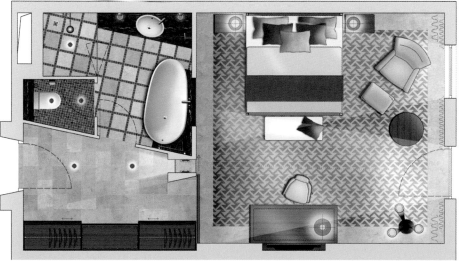

Pyramids Palace
Cairo / Egypt

Royal Suite Concept
Hotel Category: ★ ★ ★ ★ ★ superior
Hotel Type: Luxury hotel
The Brief: New building / Create a design concept for the royal suite
Floor area incl. bathrooms: 358.14 m²

Positioned on the top floor of this gigantic luxury hotel complex, the Royal Suite enjoys the best views of the Giza pyramids. The layout emphasises the flow of the rooms, from the formal reception area through to the private chambers, with separate rooms for men and women. Even the swimming facilities feature a carefully shielded private area for women.

The reception area plays a hugely important role in Arab culture. In earlier times, guests were received in lavishly decorated tents and served tea and dates while they reclined on sumptuous cushions. It was here that the councils of men met to debate important decisions. Modern buildings feature contemporary interpretations of this traditional architecture known as majlis. In the Royal Suite guests are welcomed into a formal reception area with an elevated ceiling, where carefully positioned pillars offer a glimpse of the adjoining areas. Last but not least: separate access and passageways for personnel ensure that guests can enjoy discrete and unobtrusive service at all times.

A regal atmosphere in the shadow of the pyramids.

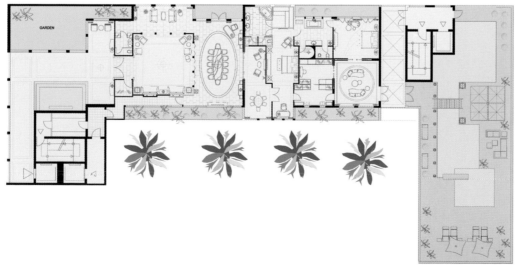

Quartier Hotel
Dresden / Germany

Room Concept
Hotel Category: ★ ★ ★ ★ ★
Hotel Type: City hotel
The Brief: New building / Create a design concept for a room
Floor area incl. bathrooms: 36.70 m²

Taking hospitality to new heights: a spacious room with an elevated ceiling! In most hotels space is at a premium and ceilings are hung accordingly low – this design takes an entirely different approach. Travellers prefer a room that features separate areas for various activities: a public area to welcome guests, a bathroom to start the day, and a sleeping area for relaxation. But where do guests go when the weather turns bad? Where do they go to stay in touch with their friends and business contacts, or just to surf the Internet? A spacious desk and easy chair have been carefully integrated into this design,

making them both a pleasure to use and a stunning visual ensemble. The reading chair adjoins the sofa arrangement, enhancing the décor of the room and adding to its aura of comfort, while the desk has been carefully positioned in a quiet zone – this a place to sit and work in peace.

A hotel with more: taking style to a higher plane.

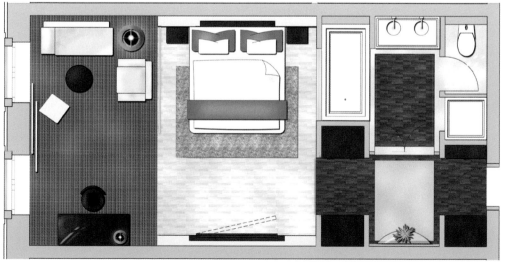

Quartier Hotel
Dresden / Germany

Junior Suite Concept
Hotel Category: ★ ★ ★ ★ ★
Hotel Type: City hotel
The Brief: New building / Create a design concept for a junior suite
Floor area incl. bathrooms: 56.45 m²

A sophisticated design: a suite that's an urban apartment. This suite is split across two levels, creating separate public and private areas.

The reception area extends through to an integrated wardrobe so that guests entering the suite will be drawn immediately to the eye-catching seating arrangement in the living area with its remarkable views of Dresden's urban landscape. Set back from the living area, the sleeping area is no less luxurious. A large, fully rotating flatscreen TV rests on three blocks of sandstone separating the two areas. Sandstone elements feature throughout the hotel, a visual reference to Dresden's famous Frauenkirche. The stone ensembles evoke images of the reconstruction of Dresden's most memorable landmark.

All too often neglected in contemporary design, the bathroom is a place of regeneration and vitality that guests will enjoy stepping into mornings and evenings. This design features a walk-in shower, separate toilet and access to the sleeping area. But the real highlight is the free-standing bathtub – simply unforgettable!

A home away from home – with plenty to discover.

Residenzhotel
Augsburg / Germany

Suite Concept
Hotel Category: ★ ★ ★ ★ ★
Hotel Type: Conference hotel
The Brief: Complete refurbishment /
Create a design concept for a suite
Floor area incl. bathrooms: 37.33 m²

Home to a substantial art collection, this historical hotel has garnered a reputation for itself as the place to celebrate anniversaries, weddings, and other important occasions on a grand scale. But the time has come for change, and the hotel is set to be completely refurbished, extended, and restructured.

The new look will marry the hotel's grand traditions with a contemporary design in which art will play a pivotal role. Some of the hotel single rooms are too small by today's standards. The solution: adjoining rooms will be connected to create suites, resulting in a spacious floor plan that meets the demands of today's discerning guests.

The bathroom's glass exterior and free-standing bathtub symbolize the dawning of a new age in this hotel. The bed rests alongside the bathroom, its frame forming a visual reference to the age of the Grand Hotel. Sliding elements enable guests to close off the public area, which includes a tribute to the hotel's art collection.

A house with a grand old tradition enters the twenty-first century.

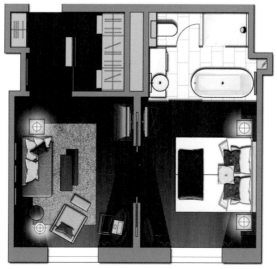

Hotel Ritter
Durbach / Germany

Comfort Room Concept
Hotel Category: ★ ★ ★ ★ superior
Hotel Type: SPA hotel
The Brief: Complete refurbishment, incl. restructuring and extensions / Create a design concept for a room
Floor area incl. bathrooms: 26.82 m²

The complete refurbishment of the rooms at this hotel was accompanied by a structural adjustment: the hotel's smallest rooms were extended by integrating the adjoining recessed balconies into the interior, creating a spacious design for today's discerning traveller. The façade was also given a complete facelift, lending the hotel a fresh, modern look, both inside and out. The new extension is modern, bright and breezy, yet also contains a key feature from the past: the wall projections have been retained and now mark off the space, creating a natural quiet zone. While few guests bring work to a wellness retreat, some might like to occasionally check their e-mails, and conference guests will find all the plugs and ports they need here. The desk may be used as a workspace but its oval form suggests pleasure rather than business. Indeed, adjoining it is an entertainment centre housing a television and hi-fi stereo – just the thing for an hour or two alone.

Turning hospitality outside in: a room with a new look.

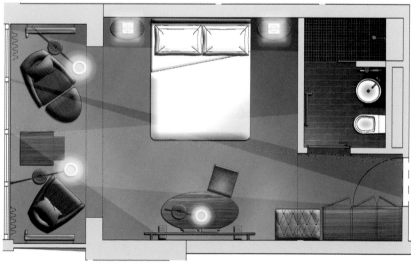

Hotel Ritter
Durbach / Germany

Junior Suite Concept
Hotel Category: ★ ★ ★ ★ superior
Hotel Type: SPA hotel
The Brief: Complete refurbishment, incl. restructuring and extensions / Create a design concept for a junior suite
Floor area incl. bathrooms: 39.33 m²

Deep in the Black Forest, nestled among the rolling hills and vineyards: this landmark institution has garnered a reputation for its gourmet food and fine wine. The main building features traditional timber framework and a spacious wine cellar, the hallmarks of southern German hospitality. This new design concept was developed following a change of ownership. The refurbishment will see the hotel's spa facilities expanded, and a new visual design with a Bacchanalian theme will be implemented throughout the hotel – including the introduction of beauty products derived from wine in the spa centre. The colour scheme sensitively inte-

grates this new design concept in the hotel's style canon: the carefully applied accents include a light green Riesling hue and a rich Pinot Noir red.

Mastering an extremely difficult balancing act, this design brings the hotel into the twenty-first century while retaining the traditional flair that has delighted so many regular customers. In this room a tailor-made art concept makes all the difference: patterns from the original wallpapering have been reinterpreted in images throughout the room.

The patterns of the past – a wallpaper design enjoys a rare comeback.

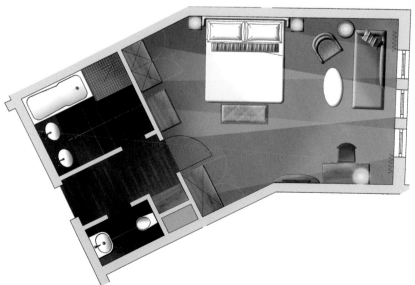

Hotel Ritter
Durbach / Germany

SPA Suite Concept
Hotel Category: ★ ★ ★ ★ superior
Hotel Type: SPA hotel
The Brief: Complete refurbishment, incl. restructuring and extensions / Create a design concept for a SPA suite
Floor area incl. bathrooms: 73.87 m²

What would a wellness hotel be without a dedicated wellness suite? This suite is equipped with its very own spa facilities, enabling couples to enjoy all the luxury of a first class spa in the privacy of their own suite. Guests can slip out of the private sauna and into bed for a nap, or relax together in front of the fire. Endless luxury: enjoy a professional massage treatment in the privacy of your suite.

A refurbished maisonette room houses one of the spa suites, comprising a public area on the lower level and private rooms above. The upper floor features a vaulted ceiling with exposed timber framework. To ensure that guests sleeping alone in the double bed don't feel lonely, the bed was designed as a modern take on the classic four-poster bed, offering a warm, protective atmosphere. The crowning detail is the knob mounted on the headboard, fashioned from the neck of a wine bottle; pull on it to play a lullaby that will sooth guests into a peaceful slumber.

Childhood memories: lullabies and sweet dreams.

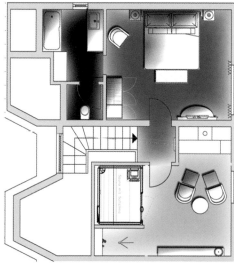

River Lounge Hotel
Prague / Czech Republic

Room Concept
Hotel Category: ★ ★ ★ ★ ★ superior
Hotel Type: City hotel
The Brief: Conversion of an existing hospital into a hotel / Create a design concept for a room
Floor area incl. bathrooms: 37.96 m²

Prague – the city of exquisite glassware and Art Nouveau! These two aspects of Prague's rich artistic heritage have been subtly incorporated into the design of this luxury hotel room.

An organic motif softens the clear lines of the functional layout: the leaf motif frames the bed and desk, and adorns the floor, walls and ceiling. Hushed shades of brown and grey contrast with a warm shade of blood orange red. The red tone underscores the elegance of the bedside pendulum lamps and the fragmented patterns that the glass lampshades cast on the walls.

Time to relax: the sofa is couched in an elegant alcove that is framed with stunning wood panelling – an ideal place to take shelter from the world, lie down, and unwind. The sofa is almost as long as a standard bed and could easily sleep a child overnight. A lighting slit between the shower and the living area connects these two zones and creates an air of spaciousness.

A room for Prague: a haven for big-city nomads.

196

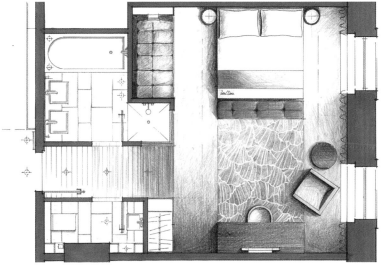

Robinson Club Fleesensee
Göhren-Lebbin, Germany

Room Concept
Hotel Category: ★ ★ ★ ★
Hotel Type: Resort hotel
The Brief: New building / Create a design concept for a room
Floor area incl. bathrooms: 36.32 m^2

An homage to nature: Germany's first Robinson Club! The interior design of each Robinson Club hotel reflects the customs and traditions of its setting, and this hotel is no exception. Discover the pristine environment of the Mecklenburg Lake District. Guests can enjoy a round of golf, go horse riding, windsurfing or sailing, play tennis or explore the region on a motorcycle. Easily accessible from both Berlin and Hamburg, Robinson Club Fleesensee is far enough from the hustle and bustle of the big city to ensure that guests can unwind and enjoy their holiday. And what does German architecture look like? The exterior and interior designs feature traditional German timber framework, inviting guests to immerse themselves in the rustic tranquillity of the Lake District. The clear lines of the rooms create a spacious effect – this is the perfect setting for a holiday, whether guests fill their days with sports or just lie back and take it easy.

Nature at its purest: relax amid down-to-earth design.

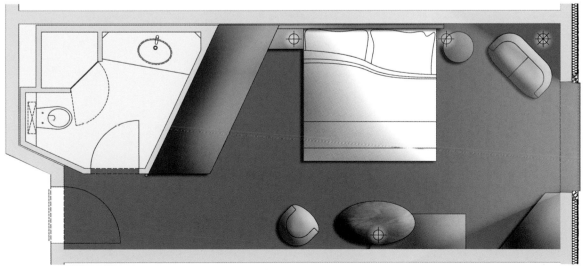

Schlosshotel Taunus
Oberursel / Germany

Room Concept
Hotel Category: ★ ★ ★ ★ superior
Hotel Type: Conference hotel
The Brief: Complete refurbishment and construction /
Create a design concept for a room
Floor area incl. bathrooms: 24.53 m²

Nature laid the foundations for this design. Located high in the mountains, the castle enjoys excellent views of the Taunus Valley and is the perfect location for high-powered conferences. Far removed from the hustle and bustle of the big city, business guests can meet in a concentrated atmosphere or just unwind and take things slowly before the backdrop of these stunning surroundings. The interior design takes its cue from the historical building and plays with motifs drawn from the region.

The rooms offer everything a guest could require, and have an individual character that is rooted in this special location. The large desk offers a generous work space, while an armchair and ottoman wait nearby for when the day's work is done. Suitably positioned, the armchair invites guests to enjoy a book or just take in the view and let their thoughts wander. The different-sized picture frames mounted on the rear wall underscore the casual and homely spirit of this room.

In nature's footsteps: A hotel room that makes the most of its surroundings.

Schlosshotel Taunus
Oberursel / Germany

Suite Concept
Hotel Category: ★ ★ ★ ★ superior
Hotel Type: Conference hotel
The Brief: Complete refurbishment and construction / Create a design concept for a suite
Floor area incl. bathrooms: 81.52 m²

With its ingenious design, this large suite offers stunning views of the Taunus Mountains from two different parts of the suite. Vaulted ceiling panels on the upper floor create a truly unique spatial experience. The layout of the floor plan separates the public and private areas, creating a flow throughout the suite that makes the most of the extraordinary views. The angled walls open up the space around the bed and make room for an additional attraction: a free-standing bath that invites guests to while away an hour gazing out of the window. A walk-in wardrobe area leads through to a separate toilet and the bath-room is located opposite. The large table in the foyer is ideal either for an informal breakfast or private meeting.

The range of materials employed in this design reflects the underlying themes: reserved natural colours form the base, while dark red accents evoke the castle's rich history. Rustic parquet flooring throughout the suite enhances the flow from one room to the next, while oval islands round off the design and identify the quiet zones.

A hotel in a castle – an encounter with history.

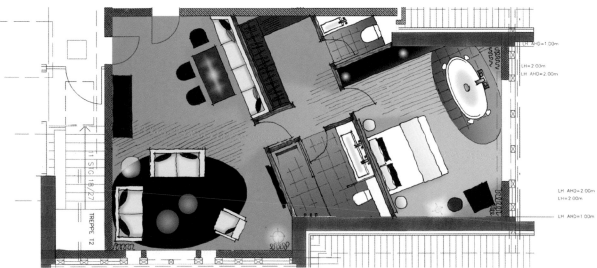

Seeresidenz
Binz on the Island of Rügen / Germany

Room Concept
Hotel Category: ★ ★ ★ ★
Hotel Type: Resort hotel
The Brief: Complete refurbishment / Create a design concept for a room
Floor area incl. bathrooms: 34.80 m²

With its chalk cliffs, tree-lined avenues and pristine white spa architecture, Rügen has plenty to offer. Situated in the north-east of Germany, this island gets its share of stormy weather, but this is more than compensated for by the luxurious spa facilities at many of the island's hotels.

Guests to this hotel can relax in a spa bath, swim in the pool, warm up in the sauna, or treat themselves to a soothing massage. However, nobody likes to spend their entire holiday in the public eye, and German holidaymakers often retreat to the privacy of a Strandkorb, the traditional wicker beach chair.

The room design concept brings the beach chair inside: the pastel colour scheme is the perfect backdrop for a relaxing day indoors. The bed is snugly couched in an alcove – a modern take on the iconic Strandkorb.

The colour scheme features a light cream tone alongside a delicate shade of blue. The flowing lines of the furnishings capture the motion of the waves, while the linear pattern and texture of the carpeting is reminiscent of windswept dunes.

A room like a day at the seaside.

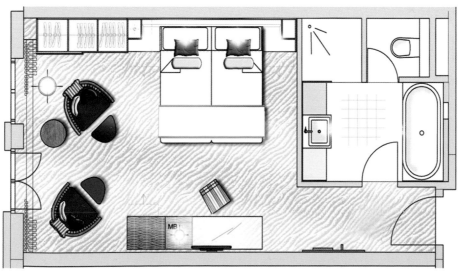

Luxury Ski Resort
Bukovel / Ukraine

Room Concept

Hotel Category: ★ ★ ★ ★ ★ superior

Hotel Type: Ski hotel

The Brief: New building / Create a design concept for a guest room

Floor area incl. bathrooms: 33.69 m²

In this high-class hotel, set deep in a forest, you can hear the mountains calling. Naturally, hotel guests expect to feel nature when they stay here, even inside the building. Natural materials create a warm and cosy atmosphere, while earthy tones give the guest an authentic sense of being in nature. Earthiness is combined with luxury through the sparkle of crystal – which is also reminiscent of snow and ice, reflecting the main theme of the hotel. The room radiates simple elegance, allowing the natural materials to dominate. The entire hotel emphasises a return to sensory impressions. It opens up time for discovery and introspection. As soon as they enter the room, guests encounter a spacious four-piece bathroom, including a separate toilet. A back-lit privacy wall made of two glass sheets with end-grain wood between the bathroom and sleeping areas allows silhouettes to be seen, but hides everything else. Daylight streams into the washing area. Parquet flooring is paired with natural stone in the bath, and a comfy woollen rug in the sitting area keeps out the winter chill.

A room you can feel – a tactile adventure.

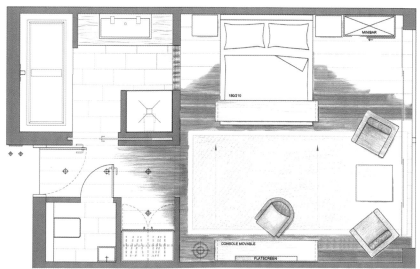

MINIBAR

180/210

CONSOLE MOVABLE

FLATSCREEN

Suite Concept

Hotel Category: ★ ★ ★ ★ ★ superior

Hotel Type: Ski hotel

The Brief: New building /
Design concept for a suite

Floor area incl. bathrooms: 50.19 m²

Building on the existing design, the junior suite features straight lines and natural surface structures. A sense of spaciousness is combined with separately zoned public and private areas. A glass partition seems almost to hang from the ceiling, yet creates an intimate mood. The integrated flat screen TV rotates to face either bed or sitting area. The entrance area features a separate toilet with bidet and sink. Opposite is a wardrobe, essential for a skiing holiday. This example features two built-in closet units.

The main bathroom is accessible from the sleeping area, with a bathtub, shower, and large double sink that allows ample space for toiletries. A recurring theme in all rooms is the translucent wall made of two glass sheets with end-grain wooden discs. The desk is small, appropriately for a resort hotel, and can also double as a make-up table with mirror. Breakfast in bed is made easy by the bed table on wheels, which can also be rolled against the glass partition and used as a sideboard.

Close to nature: mountains (almost) near enough to touch.

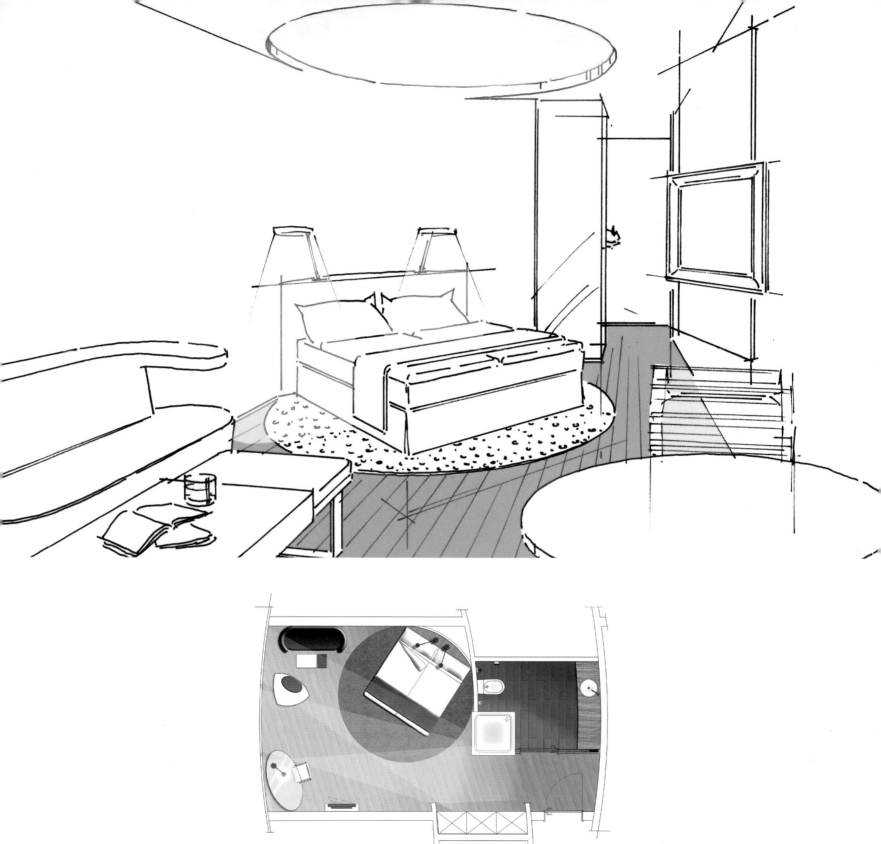

Stadtpalais Leipzig
Leipzig / Germany

Room Concept
Hotel Category: ★ ★ ★ ★ ★ superior
Hotel Type: Grand Hotel
The Brief: Remove the core of the existing townhouse and transform the property into a luxury hotel / Create a design concept for a room
Floor area incl. bathrooms: 34.48 m²

A trade fair town of old, the city of Leipzig still stands for trade and commerce, and is closely associated with the cultural and artistic legacies of Goethe and Bach, both of whom lived and worked here for a time. The building is located in the inner city, a stone's throw from several important sites in German cultural history.

The floor plan of the room focuses on the window, with the bed positioned in the centre of the room, facing the large window. The carpeting is decorated with a map of the city, identifying the hotel's location and helping visitors find their bearings. The free-standing bath will dazzle guests with its panoramic views of the city's historical architecture. Numerous details in the furnishings refer to Leipzig's role as a publishing centre – most noticeably, a book describing in detail the view from this very window and offering guests a wealth of information on the city and plenty of sightseeing ideas is 'embedded' in the oversized window frame.

A hotel room with a strong and deep connection to the city of Leipzig.

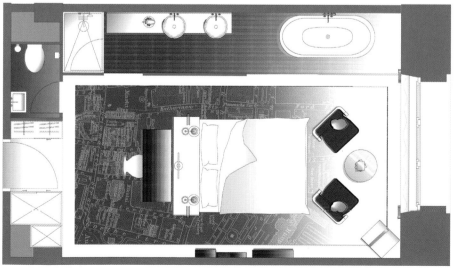

Steigenberger Grandhotel
Heringsdorf on the Island of Usedom / Germany

Room Concept
Hotel Category: ★ ★ ★ ★ ★ superior
Hotel Type: Resort hotel
The Brief: New building / Create a design concept for a room
Floor area incl. bathrooms: 35.38 m²

Located directly adjacent to the promenade, this hotel enjoys magnificent sea views, and its dazzling white façade conjures up visions of a past age of splendour! Inside guests will revel in the luxury and timeless elegance of this contemporary design. The casual "maritime chic" of the hotel reflects the island of Usedom's tasteful style: both elegant and rustic at once, this is a seaside resort par excellence. With its warm and intimate atmosphere, this is a Grand Hotel where guests will instantly feel at ease!

The room is a private refuge – a place to quietly relax with a book after a day at the beach. Double doors open onto the bathroom from the living area, revealing the interior like a jewellery box. The heirloom style of the furnishings enhances the homely atmosphere: this is like a private living room at the seaside. While a television is a necessary ingredient in any hotel room, it can intrude on the visual design – here the television has been carefully integrated through the use of an elegant frame.

Maritime elegance on Usedom.

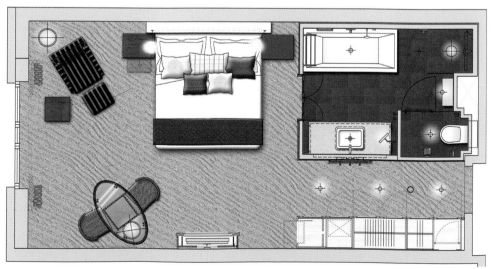

Steigenberger Grandhotel
Heringsdorf on the Island of Usedom / Germany

'Baltic' Apartment Concept
Hotel Category: ★ ★ ★ ★ ★ superior
Hotel Type: Resort hotel
The Brief: New building / Create a design concept for a serviced apartment
Floor area incl. bathrooms: 73.32 m²

There's nothing quite like the seaside, so why not stay for a while? These superior rooms are like a home away from home, with all the amenities of a modern hotel: restaurants, bars, and a range of spa facilities, including an outdoor pool. Enjoy the peace of your own private haven or mingle with other holidaymakers whenever you feel the urge! These rooms are right by the water – guests will be lulled to sleep by the sound of ocean waves gently lapping at the shoreline! And what's more - the promenade is just a few steps away!
Typical of the resorts along the German Baltic coast the Steigenberger Grandhotel in Heringsdorf combines casual elegance with an aura of seclusion and privacy. The open plan living and dining areas feature an open fireplace, while the bathroom contains a private sauna. The white stained wood furnishings and fixtures reflect the architecture of the Imperial Baths, while a splash of blue adds a maritime flair that is carefully balanced with a delicate shade of orange. Take a deep breathe, relax, and recharge your batteries.

Baltic design: seaside living.

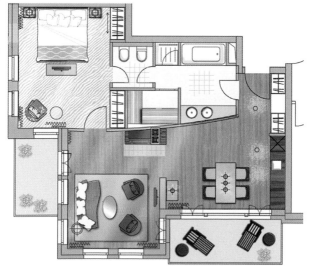

Steigenberger Hotel Treudelberg
Hamburg / Germany

Room Concept
Hotel Category: ★ ★ ★ ★ superior
Hotel Type: Urban resort hotel
The Brief: New building, extension /
Create a design concept for a room
Floor area incl. bathrooms: 33.81 m²

This is rural chic in a metropolitan oasis. The addition of a new building housing 90 rooms and suites along with additional conference and catering facilities as well as a special new spa treatment area has significantly expanded this first-class hotel for golf and conference guests.

The Mediterranean flair of the rooms in the original building has been preserved and the design for the new building draws on this style to offer an elegantly casual interpretation of country living without referring to traditional clubhouse designs. A down-to-earth design that conveys all the luxury of a five-star hotel in a sleek, cosy,

and contemporary look: dark oak, deep club armchairs, tartan patterned carpeting and dark red accents.

The almost quadratic geometry of the floor plan is balanced by the use of two different flooring materials, separating the living and sleeping areas and giving the room the feel of a junior suite. Ideally suited for high-powered conference guests and weary golfers alike, this reserved design welcomes guests with a warm embrace and an intimate atmosphere.

Laid-back elegance: a home away from home.

Steigenberger Hotel Treudelberg
Hamburg / Germany

SPA Suite Concept
Hotel Category: ★ ★ ★ ★ superior
Hotel Type: Urban resort hotel
The Brief: New building, extension /
Create a design concept for a SPA Suite
Floor area incl. bathrooms: 61.26 m²

After a day on the golf course, guests booking into the Wellness Suite at the Steigenberger Hotel Treudelberg Hamburg can unwind in a private sauna before spending a relaxing hour in a private spa pool. A private masseuse is also on hand to provide relaxing massage treatments in the suite ... if the soothing design hasn't already done the trick!

This design is everything a client could wish for – no less and no more. The suite features private wellness facilities (and is conveniently situated within one of Hamburg's top spas), a generously proportioned bathroom, and an open plan design

for maximum transparency (a principle that was applied in all 90 rooms). The living area is spacious, with plenty of room to entertain friends who might drop by for a chat or a quiet nightcap. This is a place to relax, talk in a casual atmosphere, and enjoy life. Unwind in an atmosphere of sumptuous elegance – a suite for guests who wish to treat themselves to a truly unique wellness experience.

Sanus per aquam: health by water.

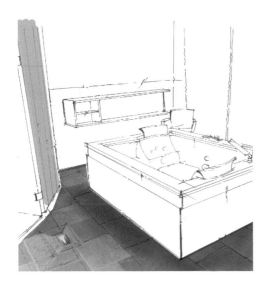

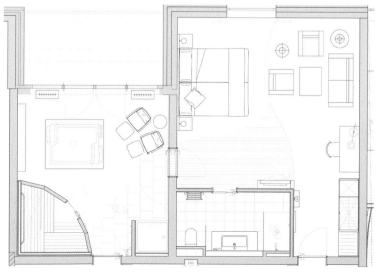

Thermenhotel
Bad Schallerbach / Austria

Room Concept
Hotel Category: ★ ★ ★ ★ ★
Hotel Type: SPA and conference hotel
The Brief: Complete refurbishment /
Create a design concept for a room
Floor area incl. bathrooms: 34.16 m^2

Health, spa, feng shui, nature, free forms, and dynamics: these are the key terms in this hotel design concept. This is a different kind of wellness resort that, thanks to its proximity to the thermal springs, offers a variety of spa therapies, inviting guests to regenerate their bodies, minds, and spirits, and to discover new élan. The design concept is unconventional, with curved flowing walls and an open bathroom area, whose centrepiece is a translucent, conical shower cabinet.

Plants next to the bed – which guests tend to for the duration of their stay – and a spacious balcony create an immediate connection to the verdant beauty and natural energy of Upper Austria. In keeping with the concepts of feng shui, the soft, flowing forms allow chi energy to flow freely, unconsciously charging guests with positive energy. Further health-inducing features include mattresses that facilitate magnetic field therapies, a bathtub with underwater speakers and coloured lighting to maximise relaxation, and variable room lighting that allows guests to adjust the lighting intensity and colour to match their emotional state.

Positive energy in a wellness resort.

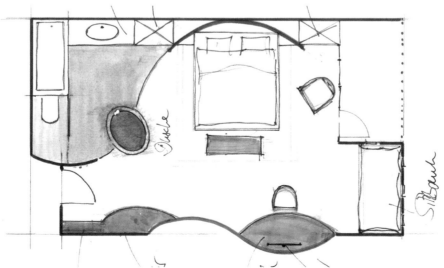

TUI Hotel
Kaluga, Russia

Room Concept
Hotel Category: ★ ★ ★ ★
Hotel Type: Business hotel
The Brief: New building / Create a design concept for a room
Floor area incl. bathrooms: 23.59 m²

Kaluga – a central hub of the Russian automotive industry located south of Moscow – was recently selected by Europe's largest tour operator as the launching pad for its new business hotel brand. The hotel is a relaxing oasis and sports a modern design with a warm colour scheme – a place of calm retreat in this industrial centre.

The design of the rooms is light, fresh, and clear. A zesty shade of green adds a splash of colour that guests will be glad to come home to after a long day at the office or production plant. The champagne-coloured mini-bar with its grass-green shelf slots onto the fitted wardrobe, forming an easily accessible (and no doubt profitable) eyecatcher.

This sleek modern design includes a number of elements that celebrate the Russian spirit – the skilfully turned table legs, for instance, neatly set off the clear lines of this design. These little surprises infuse the modern design with a charming authenticity and warmth that captures the very essence of the "Russian soul".

A refreshing design for Russia's Motor City.

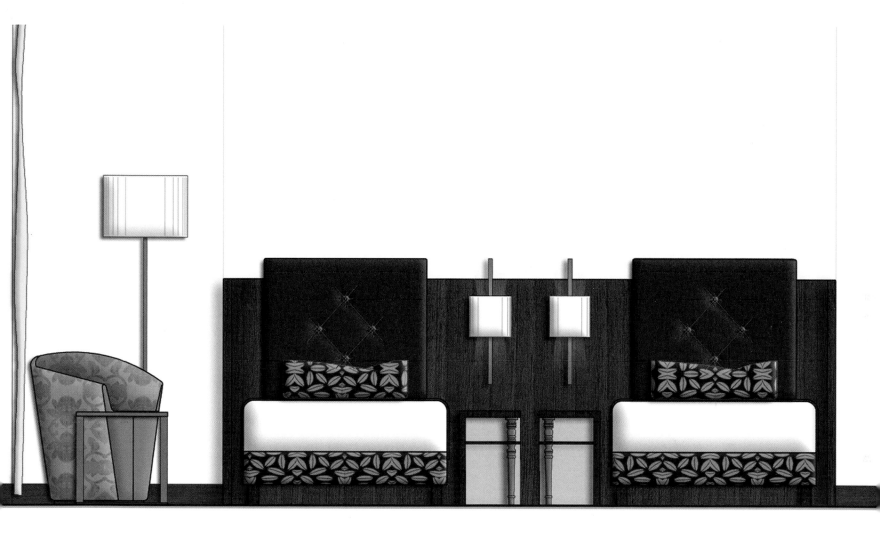

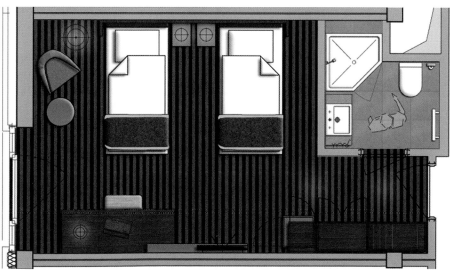

Wellnesshotel
Monschau / Germany

Room Concept
Hotel Category: ★ ★ ★ – ★ ★ ★ ★
Hotel Type: Spa and conference hotel
The Brief: New building / Create a design concept for a room
Floor area incl. bathrooms: 24.89 m²

Heavily influenced by the hotel's rural setting in central Germany, this design makes a bold statement. While many of the local hotels subscribe to a more conservative style, this project is refreshingly unique – mixing elements from several different eras, the design marries traditional German motifs with a modern ambience to achieve a contemporary space that demonstrates a healthy sense of humour.

The hotel mixes the obligatory roaring stags and garden gnomes with cubic design elements and hi-tech materials. But nature also has its place in a hotel that is firmly rooted in its rustic setting: the generous use of wood, curving forms and a warm colour scheme throughout reflect the beauty of this location. The words printed here and there on the walls of the room have a clear message: this is a design that refuses to take itself seriously. This hotel will delight and intrigue guests with its disarming style.

A tongue-in-cheek design: the hotel room as a bridge between now and then.

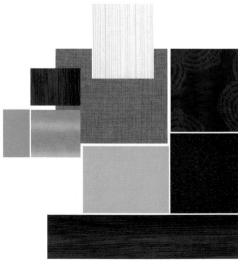

Westend Tower
Zurich / Switzerland

Room Concept
Hotel Category: ★ ★ ★ ★ ★
Hotel Type: City hotel
The Brief: New building / Create a design concept for a room
Floor area incl. bathrooms: 30.91 m²

A new first-class hotel is set to make its mark in Zurich's hippest suburb. Once an urban industrial area, Zurich West has reinvented itself as a popular entertainment district – a place to dress up and paint the town red, far removed from the Bahnhofstrasse and Lake Zurich. Innovative design concepts have transformed the suburb's legacy of industrial architecture into an eclectic wonderland: juxtaposing chandeliers with bare concrete walls, and glass and steel structures with brickwork façades.

This hotel epitomises the best of Swiss design and is destined to make its mark on the international stage. This is a modern hotel with a local touch: Swiss style, made in Zurich! The light-hearted design takes a mischievous sideways glance at Swiss traditions all the while ensuring that the end result is one of refined sophistication. The sculptural form of the bathroom's glossy crème exterior leans into the room like a mountain peak, guiding guests into the quiet zone with its leather wing chair and fur rug.

A touch of Swiss charm: a hotel for Zurich!

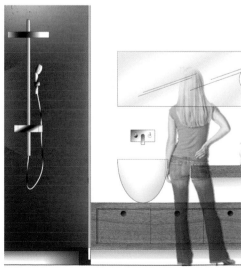

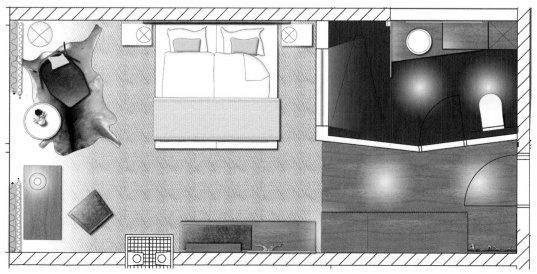

Interior Design Conception and Authors

Corinna Kretschmar-Joehnk
managing director

- born on November 4th, 1966 in Bielefeld
- school attendance in Detmold - high school diploma 1986
- study of art history in Würzburg 1986
  study of interior design in Detmold - degree (diploma) 1993
- employee at joehnk. Interior Design in Hamburg 1993,
  project manager 1996, head of catering trade dept. 1999
- manager of joehnk. Interior Design AG Zurich 2000
- manager of JOI-Design GmbH in Hamburg since 2003
- member of the BDIA since 2004
- member of the executive committee BDIA Landesverband Küste (HH, SH, MeckPom) 2004 –
  2006, today engaged in the advisory board of the executive committee BDIA LV Küste
- member in the architectural association Hamburg since 2004
- appointment to the independent inscription committee of the architectural association
  Hamburg / interior design department since 2007

Peter Joehnk
managing director

- born on July 31st, 1957 in Kronach/Ofr.
- school attendance in Selb/Ofr. and Neustadt/Wstr., high school diploma 1976
- study of interior design in Kaiserslautern and Mainz, diploma 1981
- degree of correspondence course in ecological building 1983
- formation of his own company 1984
- university teaching position at the Muthesius School, Kiel (FH)
- member of the BDIA since 1982, from 2001 until 2003 appointed as a member of the
  executive committee of the BDIA
- delegate of the BDIA in the IFI, International Federation of Interior Designers
- approval of the ECIA (European Council of Interior Architects)
- admittance as "Member of Chartered Society of Designers" MCSD, London, 1997
- election as professional of the IIDA „International Interior Designer Association" 1998
- member in the architectural association Hamburg since 1986, in the architectural association Bavaria since 1998 and in the architectural association Austria since 1996
- contest committee of the architectural association Hamburg 2000
- manager of JOI-Design GmbH in Hamburg, self-employed since 1984
- appointment to the "Konvent der Baukultur 2010"

www.JOI-Design.com

Picture Credit

p. 46 Dolce Hotel Munich

p. 76 Arnulf Hettrich

p. 92 Hilton Hotel Frankfurt-Airport

p. 154 Peters Design

p. 158 NH Hotel Frankfurt Niederrad

p. 190–194 Hotel Ritter Durbach

p. 224 TUI AG Hannover

All other pictures were made available by JOI-Design.

Imprint

The Deutsche Nationalbibliothek lists this publication in the Deutsche Nationalbibliografie; detailed bibliographical data are available on the internet at http://dnb.d-nb.de.

ISBN 978-3-03768-071-1

© 2011 by Braun Publishing AG
www.braun-publishing.ch

1st edition 2011
Translation:
Stephen Roche
Graphic concept and layout:
Michaela Prinz

All of the information in this volume has been compiled to the best of the editors knowledge. It is based on the information provided to the publisher by the architects' and designers' offices and excludes any liability. The publisher assumes no responsibility for its accuracy or completeness as well as copyright discrepancies and refers to the specified sources (architects' and designers' offices). All rights to the photographs are property of the photographer (please refer to the picture credits).